ACTIVATE
YOUR
UNLIMITED
POWER

ACTIVATE YOUR UNLIMITED POWER

DISCOVER THE BOUNDLESS POSSIBILITIES THAT LIE WITHIN

BRIAN SCOTT

ADVANCED SUCCESS
INSTITUTE

Published by Advanced Success Institute

Printed in the United States.

Paperback: 979-8-9909081-9-2

Hardcover: 979-8-9909081-1-6

E-Book: 979-8-9909081-0-9

Audio: 979-8-9909081-2-3

Dedication

This is dedicated to my wife, who supported me through this entire process. To Hayden and Hunter, who helped give me the confidence to keep going, to The Reality Revolution family for supporting me, and to Melissa, who helped give birth to this book.

TABLE OF CONTENTS

INTRODUCTION

I am Brian Scott. It has been four years since my first book, "The Reality Revolution: The Mind Blowing Movement To Hack Your Reality," was published. The response to the first book was nothing short of phenomenal, a testament to the thirst we all share for understanding the deeper truths of our existence and our capabilities to transform not just our lives but the very fabric of reality itself.

For six years, through the daily podcast "The Reality Revolution," I have explored new frontiers of thought, delving into the vast expanse of human potential, spirituality, quantum physics, and the art of manifesting the reality we desire. Each new video and meditation have been a step further into the unknown, guided by the incredible responses and transformative stories you share, the listeners and readers who have dared to dream with me.

"Activate Your Unlimited Power" is born from this incredible journey and the evolution of knowledge we've embarked on together. I was inspired after reading many classic books like "In Tune With The Infinite" by Ralph Waldo Trine, "Think And Grow Rich" by Napoleon Hill, and "The Power Of Your Subconscious Mind" by Joseph Murphy. These books will be classics hundreds of years from now. There are universal truths that are ageless that cannot be denied contained in this book. If you hold this book hundreds of years from now, you will find the same universal truths.

As my channel has evolved and my understanding of language and trance induction is being enhanced, I have learned how to do something I like to call an activation. I have carefully crafted these words to move beyond your conscious mind and activate programs within your subconscious. This book is an activation and the very process of reading will trigger this activation. You will feel this change and begin to see it with each page you read.

The magic comes from believing in the unlimited power of your mind and experiencing the changes that manifest when you truly embrace the idea that you create your reality.

In this book, I invite you to go further, to let go of the past, recognize and embrace your inherent magnificence, and wield your magnetic nature. Together, I will explore new dimensions of what it means to bring magic into your life, to live as if limits are but illusions, and to manifest the reality that resonates with the deepest parts of your soul.

My goal is to refine the techniques and insights that will allow you to tap into the infinite well of potential within.

Welcome to the next phase of The Reality Revolution.

CHAPTER ONE

THERE IS NO LIMIT

"There is one grand lie – that we are limited. The only limits we have are the limits we believe."

—*Wayne Dyer*

It is natural to think that the world is limited. You have experienced limits during every step of your life. From the moment you are born, you are introduced to a world of limits—both physical and conceptual. You are confined by your body. As an infant, you cannot walk, talk, or feed yourself; you are reliant on others for survival. Early on, our understanding of the world is incredibly limited, shaped by immediate sensations and experiences. From emotions to language, we are taught that the universe is limited. This limited understanding is programmed into us.

This book aims to create a new belief that there is no limit to the miracles you can create when you activate your unlimited power. I speak from experience. I have seen the most miraculous things transpire. I've seen people overcome everything you can imagine: extreme poverty, life-threatening obesity, terminal cancer, you name it. If you can grasp this concept and wield the unlimited power you can access now, your life will be magical. There is absolutely no limit to what you can achieve.

By understanding this limitless source of power, you can perceive the very essence of your potential. You stand at the crossroads of possibility, where the boundaries of what you can achieve are not dictated by the world around you but are sculpted by the power of your mind and your brain; these intricate networks of neurons are like the universe itself, vast, complex, and largely uncharted, every thought, every dream, and every moment of inspiration is a spark in the cerebral universe, and what fuels the sparks you experience. Your boundless imagination, the ability to transcend the here and now to envision worlds beyond the tangible, the immediate, and the real, creates miracles.

History whispers tales of the impossible made possible, from the Wright Brothers taking to the skies to the incredible lunar landing, from the ancient pyramids to modern marvels of technology. At one point, these were all figments of imagination, dreams deemed too lofty and too far-fetched. Yet here we are, living in a world transformed by those very dreams.

What are limits? Are they not merely illusions, shadows cast by your doubts and fears? Every limit in history was a barrier waiting to be broken, a challenge awaiting its champion. When Roger Bannister broke the four-minute mile, a feat once thought physically impossible for humans; he didn't just surpass a physical barrier; he shattered a mental blockade. His feet were a testament to the power of belief, a demonstration that limits are often self-imposed. Thereafter, once Bannister broke the four-minute mile, many others did as well.

REALIZING UNLIMITED GROWTH

Each one of us has faced moments where the horizon of our potential seems distant and even unattainable. Have you found yourself saying,

"There's no way I can do that," or "That is impossible?" What is it that propels us forward? It is the resilience of this human spirit. The unyielding belief that there is more, that we are more in our quest for growth.

The only ceilings for self-actualization are those you place over yourself in recognizing your limitless potential. Let's not forget the power of community. You are a social being interconnected in an intricate web of relationships and influences. You amplify your potential by uplifting others and sharing your collective dreams and aspirations. The synergy of collaborative minds is a force multiplier in our journey toward breaking barriers, winning, and failing along the way. Failure is not the antithesis of success. It is its companion; each stumble and each fall is not a limit. It is a lesson, a stepping stone to achieving the extraordinary.

The future is an open canvas, and you are the artist; together, we are painting a world of endless potential with every brushstroke of innovation and every color of creativity. Dream, dare, defy, and challenge the status quo—question, be impossible, and embrace the unknown. When your mind says, "That's impossible; I am limited," you must reverse that thought. From the vast expanse of human potential, there truly is no limit.

Embark on this journey with an open heart and mind, and unlock the infinite possibilities that await you. If you can grasp this belief that there is no limit, it will ignite a transformation, a revolution of self. I'm not asking you to talk about this or think about it but to **become the embodiment of it**. There is no limit. It's a powerful truth. The foundation of all achievement is belief. It's not the circumstances nor the resources but the resourcefulness fueled by belief that creates extraordinary lives.

Believe in the limitless power of your potential. When you truly believe, there is a shift from impossibility to possibility. Consider the stories of people who have achieved the impossible. They weren't superhuman. They were individuals who harnessed the power of belief. They saw no limits, only challenges to be overcome. Their stories are not just narratives. They are the blueprints for us to follow. Every limit you face is an opportunity to grow stronger, wiser, and more resilient. When you confront your limits, you get to know your true self.

Decide now to break through every barrier that holds you back.

What is holding you back?

What is your obstacle?

Obstacles are not dead ends. They are detours on the path to your greatness. Transform your obstacles into stepping stones. Change your perspective. Ask yourself how this challenge can serve your growth. With this mindset, every obstacle becomes a tool for empowerment. It's not just about knowing that there are no limits. It's about living it. Action is the bridge between the internal world of belief and the external world of achievement.

Often, a belief that you are limited and that what you want is impossible stops you from taking action. But the truth is massive, determined action is the key. Start small if you have to. Your mind and body are interconnected.

YOUR PHYSIOLOGY CAN SHAPE YOUR PSYCHOLOGY

Do you want to feel limitless? Adopt a posture of confidence. Breathe with limitlessness and move with purpose. Let your body tell your mind that you are ready for greatness. Vision is seeing the invisible and believing in its possibility. When you create a compelling vision for your life, when you create a vision that excites you, that gets you up in the morning with enthusiasm, your vision becomes a compass guiding you through the seas of life toward your dreams. But if you believe that it's impossible, that there are limits to what you envision, it will never come to pass. True fulfillment comes when you transcend yourself. It comes from growth and contribution. Ask yourself, "How can I grow? How can I contribute?" In contribution, you find meaning; in growth, you break the chains of limitation.

Remember this moment, right now, as the beginning of your new journey, an adventure where you embrace the belief that there is no limit. Take this energy, this fire within you, and let it fuel your path toward an extraordinary life.

YOU HAVE THE POWER

Go out there and show the world that, indeed, there is no limit to what you can achieve. Are you still doubting that there is no limit? Pick up your Bible. There's profound wisdom in the scriptures that explores the idea that all things are possible and there are no limits to what you can achieve. This concept is deeply rooted in spiritual understanding and reveals how the power of belief and imagination are instrumental in shaping your reality.

- **"Jesus said unto him, if thou canst believe, all things are possible to him that believeth."** —Mark 9:23

  This powerful declaration was not just an assurance; it was an invitation by Jesus to step into a realm where your power of belief transcends the boundaries of the physical world. To believe in limitlessness is to open the door to infinite possibilities. With this understanding, you must acknowledge that your perceived limits are often self-imposed.

- **"Now, faith is the substance of things hoped for, for the evidence of things not seen."** —Hebrews 11:1

  Faith, in essence, is the bridge between your current reality and the unseen, limitless world of possibilities. Through the creative act of imagination, we give substance to our hopes and dreams by visualizing and believing in a desired outcome. By aligning yourself with the limitlessness of the universe, you will manifest whatever you want.

- **"As a man thinketh in his heart, so is he."** —Proverbs 23:7

  This is a profound piece of wisdom, underscoring your mind's transformative power. Our outer reality is a reflection of our inner world. And by cultivating limitless beliefs in our hearts and minds, we shape the course of our lives.

- **"And all things, whatsoever ye shall ask in prayer, believing, ye shall receive."** —Matthew 21:22

Prayer, in this context, is more than a petition. It is an active, creative process that involves asking and believing with unwavering conviction that what you seek is already yours without limits.

- **"I can do all things through Christ which strengthened me."** —Philippians 4:13

And here lies the ultimate assurance of your limitless potential. It is through your connection with the Divine, your inner spiritual strength, that you transcend limitations.

- **"But Jesus beheld them and said unto them with men, this is impossible, but with God, all things are possible."** —Matthew 19:26

Let there be no doubt that when you are aligned with the Divine will, any goal that may seem unattainable through human efforts alone can be achieved through faith and trust. In God's plan, you open yourself to a realm where limitations do not exist.

- **"And Jesus answered them with the truth, I say to you, if you have faith, and do not doubt, you will not only do what has been done to the fig tree but even if you say to this mountain, be taken up and thrown into the sea, it will happen."** —Matthew 21:21

Does this not highlight the extraordinary power of your spoken word when combined with unwavering faith? It suggests that you can bring about significant changes in your reality without limit through the strength of your convictions and the certainty of your words.

CONQUERING THE IMPOSSIBLE

Nelson Mandela once said, "It always seems impossible until it's done." These words echo a truth many of us have forgotten. What seems insurmountable today may become the benchmark of tomorrow. Mandela's life is a testament to this belief, showing us that the journey to achieving the extraordinary begins the moment we decide that the impossible is but a challenge to be met. I always hear echoes of impossibility spoken—especially when people are entrenched in the news and the latest headlines. "Oh, the Middle East conflict, it's impossible. They'll never be able to overcome that." "Cancer is impossible." "There's no way we'll ever be able to solve that." "Global warming is impossible." "We might as well just give up." "There's no way we can overcome that."

Regardless of the impossible belief, the truth is...there is no limit.

Michael Phelps, an Olympian whose achievements have etched his name in history, believed you can't put a limit on anything. The more you dream, the farther you get. His journey of relentless pursuit and unparalleled success demonstrates that your dreams are the wings upon which you ascend to heights unseen. The size of your dreams dictates the journey of your life. One of my favorites, Muhammad Ali, said,

> "Impossible is just a big word thrown around by small men who find it easier to live in the world they've been given than to explore the power they have to change it. Impossible is not a fact. It's an opinion. Impossible is not a declaration. It's a dare. Impossible is potential. Impossible is temporary. Impossible is nothing."

Ali's life was a continuous battle against the impossible, and he emerged victorious time and time again. Let his words inspire you to confront the impossible, not as a barrier, but as a challenge waiting to be conquered.

THE PSYCHOLOGY OF LIMITATION

You must understand the psychology of limitation to unlock the doors to your full potential.

As I've said, beliefs are powerful. That's because they are the lenses through which you view the world and yourself. These beliefs, especially about your capabilities, form early in life and are influenced by your experiences, societal norms, and the voices of those around you. Negative beliefs such as "I'm not good enough," "I can't do this," or "This is impossible for me" act as mental barriers. Beliefs like this create a self-fulfilling prophecy where your perceived limitations become your reality. I see it play out all the time. In most cases, people aren't even aware of it.

These limiting beliefs are often rooted in fear of the unknown, judgment, and failure. These fears are like invisible chains holding you back from exploring new opportunities, taking risks, and stepping out of your comfort zone. In its attempt to protect you, your mind ends up imprisoning you within the walls of safety and familiarity. You can overcome these mental barriers through awareness, acknowledgment, reframing things as challenges by being self-compassionate, visualization, visualizing yourself doing what you want to do, seeking evidence, and looking for evidence that contradicts your limiting beliefs.

For every thought that says, "I can't," find a counter-example where you or others have achieved similar goals. Surround yourself with people who believe in you and your potential. Seek mentorship from those who have walked a similar path. The support and wisdom of others can be powerful tools in overcoming any doubt or limitations you might have.

A study by Blackwell and Dweck illustrated how students with a fixed mindset, believing their intelligence is static, showed lower academic achievement compared to those with a growth mindset who believe intelligence can be developed.[1] Limiting beliefs can affect career progression. According to a study by Feldman in 2012, individuals who believed they had limited career potential were less likely to engage in professional development activities and take on challenging assignments, negatively impacting their career growth.[2]

The impact of limiting beliefs on mental health is well documented. For instance, a study by MacLeod and Moore in 2000 found that individuals who held pessimistic beliefs about their future were more likely to experience depression and anxiety.[3] These beliefs create a negative thought pattern that will lead to chronic stress, reduced self-esteem, and a feeling of helplessness, all of which are risk factors for mental health disorders.

These limiting beliefs can affect physical health, social relationships, and financial behavior. A 2012 study by Lusardi and Mitchell showed that individuals who believe they lack financial knowledge are less likely to engage in financial planning and sub-

---

[1] https://srcd.onlinelibrary.wiley.com/doi/abs/10.1111/j.1467-8624.2007.00995.x

[2] https://onlinelibrary.wiley.com/doi/full/10.1111/j.1744-6570.2010.01184.x

[3] https://www.researchgate.net/publication/230008928_Positive_Thinking_Revisited_Positive_Cognitions_Well-being_and_Mental_Health

optimal investment choices, leading to poor financial outcomes.[4] Many of these studies show that what you've experienced tends to be your limit. If you haven't experienced anything beyond it, then it doesn't mean it's not possible. If you've always made $50,000 a year and, in your mind, you say, "I can't make $200,000 a year," it's because you've only experienced that $50,000 range. So, you must escape from the limits of your experience. The experience that you're in right now is the key.

TRANSCENDING LIMITS THROUGH YOUR SUBCONSCIOUS MIND

Our minds are divided into the conscious and subconscious, and while the conscious mind is our reasoning and logical self, the subconscious is the bedrock of our deepest beliefs and perceptions. The seeds of unlimited potential flourish or wither away within the fertile soil of your subconscious mind. When you plant positive empowering beliefs in your subconscious, you set the stage for limitless growth.

What we firmly believe we make real in our lives. Our beliefs are like a script, and the subconscious acts as a diligent actor, playing out the scripts in the theater of your life. If your script is written with limitation and doubt, your life mirrors this limitation and doubt. However, when you rewrite these scripts to reflect abundance, success, and positivity, your life transforms to match these new beliefs. You can influence your subconscious by visualizing your goals and affirming with conviction your goals as already achieved in present time.

You can communicate directly with your subconscious, which is

---

[4] https://www.aeaweb.org/articles?id=10.1257/jel.52.1.5

the fertile ground of unlimited possibility. This process bypasses the critical filters of the conscious mind, planting the seeds of your desires deep within. When Jesus says, "All things are possible with God," he is saying that all things are possible with your subconscious mind.

Many of us have been programmed with limiting beliefs since childhood. These beliefs may stem from past failures, societal conditioning, or negative influences. But the past does not have to dictate your future. You have the power to reprogram your mind to replace limiting beliefs with empowering ones. This reprogramming is not an overnight process, but with persistence and faith, it is undoubtedly achievable.

The Law of Attraction states that like attracts like; as a result, your dominant thoughts and beliefs will attract corresponding events and circumstances into your life. By focusing your thoughts on positive outcomes, maintaining an optimistic outlook, and realizing your limitless potential, you attract positive experiences and limitless opportunities. Believe me when I tell you the only limits are those you impose upon yourself.

YOUR LIMITLESS MINDSET

Your mind is the most powerful tool at your disposal. It's the genesis of every reality that you experience. When you understand how to harness this power, you unlock doors to possibilities you never could have imagined. So, you must liberate your mind from the shackles of any limiting beliefs. What is limiting you now? What beliefs do you have that are limiting you? Creating a limitless mindset begins with awareness. Be aware of when a limiting thought comes up, and replace that limiting thought with an empowering one.

Your mind is like a vast uncharted galaxy, brimming with nebulae of ideas, planets of potential, and stars of creativity. When you look within, you realize that your imagination is boundless. It's in this internal cosmos that everything is possible. Your thoughts, dreams, and visions will always be the architects of your reality. When you embrace this, you embrace the unlimited possibilities available to you. What you can conceive, you can achieve. Imagine the ancient myths of alchemists turning lead into gold. Your mind possesses a similar alchemy, turning thoughts into reality. This magical process starts with your imagination, the ability to envision a world different from your present. But imagination alone is not enough; it must be coupled with deliberate, purposeful, and relentless action.

The future is not a distant dream; it is a present possibility. I have so many stories I can tell you about people I've met who've done the impossible. There's my friend Emily, who was diagnosed with a rare muscular disorder in her childhood. She was told she'd never be able to engage in strenuous physical activity. Instead of accepting this as her limit, she adopted her lifestyle and exercise routines to strengthen her body, and against all odds, she completed a marathon at 30, inspiring others with similar conditions. I also think of Sarah. She spent her life as a school teacher, often writing short stories in her spare time. At 62, after retiring, she decided to write a novel. Friends and family admired her passion but doubted her chances of getting published at her age. Undeterred, she persisted. Her debut novel, released when she was 65, became a bestseller. Her journey illustrates that it's never too late to pursue a dream and that age is not a barrier to success.

Take a moment and envision a future where you truly embrace your limitless potential. Adopting a limitless mindset will encourage bold, innovative thinking, breaking away from traditional methods and beliefs. We can advance and progress in science and technology, and it could lead to rapid advancements in fields like space exploration, medicine, and artificial intelligence, significantly expanding our understanding and capabilities. We can solve complex global challenges with this belief by viewing challenges such as climate change, energy scarcity, or international health crises without the constraints of current limitations.

We can inspire groundbreaking solutions by envisioning them.

A limitless perspective can drive the development of sustainable technologies and innovative strategies to tackle these critical issues. If we embrace limitlessness, it will lead to a more inclusive society by challenging and ultimately dismantling societal barriers that we thought could never be dismantled. This mindset fosters a culture that values diversity, equity, and inclusion. Educational paradigms could shift towards nurturing creativity, critical thinking, and problem-solving skills, emphasizing the belief that there are no limits to what students can learn and achieve. This change could prepare future generations for a rapidly evolving world.

AFFIRMATIONS—THERE IS NO LIMIT

Amazing things can happen in your life. I have some affirmations you can start saying to yourself to unlock the limits that you have in your life and embrace a mindset fostering a belief in infinite possibilities.

- I am limitless in my capacity for growth, success, and achievement.

- Every day, I push the boundaries of what I once thought was impossible.

- My potential is infinite and unbounded.

- I am constantly surpassing my expectations.

- I embrace challenges as opportunities to demonstrate that there are no limits to my abilities.

- I am a boundless source of creativity and innovation.

- The only limits that exist are those I choose to acknowledge; therefore, I choose limitlessness.

- I am constantly expanding my horizons and breaking new ground in my personal and professional life.

- Limitations are merely stepping stones on my path to greatness.

- With every action, I shatter the illusion of limitation.

- The sky is not my limit. It's my playground.

- I transcend all perceived barriers, reaching new heights of success and fulfillment.

- In the realm of my mind, there are no boundaries, only opportunities for growth and innovation.

- I am the architect of my destiny, and I design it to be boundless.

- Each day, I am more powerful, more capable, and more limitless than the day before.

Repeating these affirmations will profoundly influence your subconscious mind and reprogramming to encourage a shift from a mindset of limitation to one of endless possibilities.

You are limitless, and there is no limit to what you can do. It's time to unleash your power.

CHAPTER TWO

UNLEASH YOUR POWER

"Power is not brute force and money; it is in your spirit."

— *Swami Vivekananda*

When you walk away from today, you will be aware of an electrifying truth that pulses through the very fabric of your existence. You possess within you a reservoir of power that defies comprehension, a power so potent that it can reshape the exact contours of reality itself.

In this chapter, we are going to unleash that power.

Power is a fundamental force that shapes the human condition and carves the contours of history. It is the invisible hand that orchestrates the rise and fall of empires, the silent whisper that influences personal ambitions, and the undercurrent that drives societal change. Throughout history, the pursuit of power has been a driving force behind human interactions, whether in the corridors of governments, across the battlefields of wars, or within the subtle dynamics of family relationships. Its importance lies not only in authority or control it grants but also in its ability to transform societies, innovate economies, and influence ideologies. Understanding power is essential to comprehend the complexities of human behavior and the historical events that have shaped our world.

In a world cloaked in doubt, many external voices attempt to drown out the whispers of your inner potential; you must understand that you have all the power you need. I declare that you are the creator of your destiny. I can't wait for you to become aware of the boundless possibilities as you embrace this truth.

Imagine a life unburdened by the weight of self-doubt—a life where your deepest desires and loftiest ambitions are not mere phantoms but tangible realities. Each thought, intention, and breath you take becomes a brushstroke on the canvas of your existence, and you are painting a vivid masterpiece reflecting your true power and potential. Do not be swayed by the naysayers, the skeptics, or the cynics. The power within you is as limitless as the cosmos itself. And just as the stars light up the night sky, your dreams have the power to illuminate the path ahead. When you look up into the night sky at all those stars, know you create all of it with your power. You are not a bystander in the grand spectacle of life. You are the star of your show.

Now is the time to step into the spotlight and unleash the torrent of creativity, resilience, and unwavering determination that resides within you now.

At this moment, the universe, in all its infinite wisdom, has conspired for your existence, and it beckons you to claim your birthright to seize your destiny with both hands. The adventure you're about to embark upon is not for the faint of heart. But it is worth every step, every stumble, every victory, and every defeat. It is a journey that will lead you to the essence of your being, where realizing your true power will shatter the chains of limitation and set you free.

Open your heart, mind, and soul to the revelation that awaits.

How can you not be inspired, moved, and transformed when you meditate on your inner power? As you dive into the depths of your potential, you will discover the truth echoed through the ages. You can shape your reality, conquer your fears, and achieve the extraordinary. Anything is possible for you if you tap into this limitless power within. It's time to unleash your power and redefine the essence of what it means to be alive.

BRING YOUR POWER TO LIFE

In the annals of human existence, power has perpetually coursed through the veins of your story, an undeniable current that shapes the core of civilization itself. Across the epochs, power has worn countless masks, each revealing facets of its adaptable nature, both within and without. Externally, power has manifested as kingdoms and empires as weapons as the shifting sands of the political mind, from the Pharaohs of ancient Egypt to the Emperors of Rome to the narrative history that echoes with tales of those who harnessed external power to erect great monuments and subjugate entire populations.

This external power, often fascinating in its allure, has also birthed countless conflicts, struggles, and revolutions—a tempestuous tide of human endeavor seeking equilibrium and justice. Of course, you've heard the phrase, "power corrupts," and absolute power corrupts. However, the key is to understand that this power is quite different from the power of those dictators and civilizations, for this power is much mightier.

While external power has held dominion over realms and territories, another realm beckons—one of internal power that resides within your spirit's depths. This inner sanctum, often obscured by the clamor of the external world, is where the true alchemy of existence takes place. Internally, power manifests as the flame of imagination, a potent force that ignites the human soul and propels you beyond the confines of the ordinary. It is the wellspring from which your creativity flows, birthing symphonies of our discoveries of science and revolutions of thought.

Power is not solely the province of kings and conquerors, nor is it merely the flame of artists and thinkers. It resides in the sinews of every being, a latent potential waiting to be awakened and channeled. The harmonious external and internal power convergence propels you to your highest potential. It's the force that empowers you to shape the world around you and craft the narrative of your own life.

We've witnessed the epochs of history harness and ride the waves of internal and external power, each leaving its indelible mark on human existence. The call to action is before us to recognize the boundless potential that resides within and without and to wield it with wisdom, compassion, and a profound understanding that you are not merely a passenger in this voyage but a captain and a creator.

THE DIVINE PRESENCE WITHIN

You name it, and you have the power to do it. You can create anything, you can do anything, and you can overcome anything. All the power resides within you. No matter your situation, within you is a Divine spark that echoes through the ages, waiting to be awakened.

It is a truth as old as time, rooted in the very essence of existence. A truth whispered in the ancient scriptures, echoing through the corridors of human history and sprinkled throughout the Bible to remind us of the power within.

- **"Know ye not that ye are the temple of God, and that the Spirit of God dwelleth in you?"** —1 Corinthians 3:16

  These words in the sacred texts carry a profound message of the Divine presence within you. It is a presence that transcends the limitations of the physical realm and connects you to the infinite. Your imagination, which wanders the faculty of the mind, serves as the gateway to this inner sanctum as it is written.

- **"For as he thinketh in his heart, so is he."** —Proverbs 23:7

  You hold the key to unlocking the latent power within the realm of the imagination. Here, the seeds of desire take root where visions are born, and the very fabric of reality is woven.

- **"I tell you the truth, if you had faith even as small as a mustard seed, you could say to this mountain, 'Move from here to there,' and it would move. Nothing would be impossible."** —Matthew 17:20

  The power for which I speak is not a matter of wishing or hoping. It is a matter of knowing and believing. You are a vessel of Divine power, a conduit through which the infinite expresses itself.

- **"For God hath not given us the spirit of fear, but of power, love, and a sound mind."** —2 Timothy 1:7

  Does this not emphasize that fear is not the prevailing spirit within you? Instead, you are endowed with the spirit of power. It suggests tapping into this inner power to overcome fear and make sound, empowered decisions.

- **"I can do all things through Christ, which strengthened me."** —Philippians 4:13

  When I talk about imagination, I am not talking about mere fantasy. When I use that word, many think imagination is just daydreaming. But it's not that simple. Imagination is the realm where the power of God stirs. The scriptures proclaim, "...with God, all things are possible." As you dare to imagine, you tap into the Divine wellspring, where the formless take shape and the invisible becomes visible.

- **"Ask, and it shall be given; seek and ye shall find, knock and it shall be opened unto you."** — Matthew 7:7

  This is an invitation to align your desires with the power that resides within you. Your imagination becomes the vessel through which you unleash this power. And in doing so, you manifest the power of God in your life.

Christ, according to Neville Goddard, is your imagination. Deep within the recesses of your mind lies this boundless potential. It is a realm that defies the limits of conscious thought. A place where dreams take shape and reality is fashioned. This realm is the seat of your subconscious mind. It is a wellspring of power that shapes the course of your life in profound and often unseen ways. The imagination is the subconscious acting in the conscious mind.

Consider the power of suggestion of force that penetrates the fortress of your conscious mind, taking root in the soil of the fertile subconscious when you repeatedly affirm a belief or desire. It is as though you're planting seeds in the rich earth of your subconscious each time you practice affirming your desires and beliefs. Over time, these seeds take root, sprouting into thoughts, emotions, and actions that align with your deepest convictions.

Joseph Murphy tells us that the subconscious is a faithful servant, tirelessly working to bring the reality you impress upon. The subconscious is very, very powerful because it operates according to the law of belief. If you can activate the creative power of your subconscious, ushering in a transformation, you will align your external circumstances with your internal convictions.

Recognizing that the subconscious is impartial is imperative—it responds to constructive and destructive suggestions with equal measure. If unchecked, the power of your mind can amplify your negative beliefs and doubts, and they will take root and shape your reality. You are unleashing your power with every breath. Thus, it is paramount to guard your thoughts because they mold your subconscious landscape. Harnessing the power of your subconscious requires a deliberate and disciplined approach.

YOUR INNER POWER

At its core, your inner power is about recognizing and harnessing your true potential. The inner strength fuels your dreams, the unwavering belief in your abilities, and the driving force behind your aspirations. You gain access to this inner sanctuary through meditation, visualization, and the repetition of positive affirmations. When you combine the subconscious with the power of your imagination, all things are possible, and your power is truly unleashed.

You must learn to reprogram the subconscious, replacing the limiting beliefs that take away your power. And in so doing, you unlock the gateway to untold possibilities in your power, which is not a tangible entity nor something bestowed upon a chosen few. It is inherent for everyone and is an intrinsic capacity that resides within every individual. Think of it as a life force that propels you forward. The spark of resilience that allows you to overcome adversity and the well of creativity from which your unique gifts and talents emerge.

To understand the significance of your inner power, you must acknowledge its role in your journey of personal growth. Imagine your inner power is the engine of a mighty ship, and without it, the vessel remains adrift, subject to the whims of external currents and uncertain winds. Working with your inner power, you become the captain of your destiny, charting a course toward your chosen destination in a world often characterized by external influences, societal expectations, and self-doubt. Your inner power is a beacon of guidance and self-assurance, empowering you to navigate life's stormy seas with courage, resilience, and purpose—allowing you to set sail toward your dreams even when the shores seem distant and obscured.

Self-doubt born from fear and insecurity acts as a fog that obscures your inner radiance. External influences such as societal norms and the opinions of others can serve as the weights that anchor you to conformity, deterring you from fully expressing and unleashing your unique potential. Think of a sapling growing beneath the dense canopy of a forest. Despite its potential to grow tall and reach the sky, it must contend with limited sunlight and resources. Similarly, the shadows of doubt and the weight of external expectations can stifle our inner power.

Throughout history, we find inspiring examples of individuals who tapped into their inner power to achieve remarkable success. Consider figures like Nelson Mandela, who, facing decades of imprisonment and oppression, emerged as a symbol of resilience and reconciliation. His inner power, fueled by an unwavering belief in justice and equality, propelled him to transform an entire nation. Helen Keller's story is a testament to the triumph of inner power despite being deaf and blind from a young age. Keller's indomitable spirit and determination led her to become an author, a lecturer, and an advocate for the deaf and blind community. Keller's inner power allowed her to transcend the limitations of her physical senses and inspire countless others.

In many more stories, we witnessed the transformative potential of inner power. It is a force that drives individuals to overcome seemingly insurmountable obstacles, shape their destinies, and leave an indelible mark on the world. Deep within you lies a more potent force than you could ever imagine. The power propels you to defy the odds, conquer your fears, and shatter limitations. It's a force as ancient as humanity itself. But let me be clear: tapping into this power is not just wishful thinking or daydreams. It's about a radical shift in mindset and action that transforms the ordinary into the extraordinary. You have the power to refuse to settle for mediocrity. You can wake up every morning with an unshakable belief in your ability to create the life you desire—a life where setbacks are mere stepping stones to your success.

Your curated, vibrant life is not a pipe dream. It is a reality that countless individuals have achieved throughout history. Against all odds, they have unleashed their inner power to transcend their circumstances. Take the story of Thomas Edison. He failed over 1000 times before he finally invented a lightbulb. When asked about his failures, he famously said, "I have not failed. I've just found 10,000 ways that won't work." That's the power of relentless determination and an unwavering belief in one's abilities. Of course, new thought authors like Anthony Norville and Joseph Murphy loved to mention Thomas Edison. And that's because his story is a powerful example of your inner power and the importance of never giving up after failing.

What is holding you back? What is holding your powers back? Is it doubt or past failures? Doubt, failures, and past mishaps are just illusions. These thoughts are smoke and mirrors that have no power over you unless you grant them power. You see, fear is false evidence appearing real. Doubt is merely delayed opportunity, undermining belief in triumph and failure. Consider fear and doubt as feedback and insight, leading us to evolve and rise. The power within you transcends these obstacles. It's a power that says, "I may stumble, but I will never stay down. I may face setbacks, but I will rise stronger. I may have doubts, but I will take action regardless."

So, how do you unleash this power? It starts with a decision. A commitment to yourself that you will no longer accept an ordinary life. You will no longer let fear dictate your choices and will no longer be a prisoner of your doubts. It's about setting clear, compelling goals that pull you forward and align with your deepest desires and values. It's about creating a captivating vision of the future that excites you, a vision that becomes your north star guiding your every action.

In your pursuit of greatness, surround yourself with those who elevate and challenge you to rise. Seek mentors, coaches, and role models who have walked the path you aspire to walk. Choose to learn from their wisdom and apply it to your journey, for they have unleashed their power. How can you not learn to unleash yours by watching and learning from them? Remember, your success comes back to the burning desire within you that says, "I will not settle for less than I'm capable of. I will not let fear dictate my future; I will rise and achieve my dreams."

CHALLENGING THE CHALLENGES

Life can throw some tough punches on the way to achieving your dreams. And it's easy to feel like you're at the mercy of your circumstances. You have a choice. You can let life happen to you, or you can happen to life. It starts with your mindset. You've got to believe in yourself and your abilities. As Henry Ford once said, "Whether you think you can or think you can't, you're right." Your beliefs shape your reality. So, choose to believe that you can achieve greatness.

Once you've got that vision, break it into actionable steps; small, consistent actions add significant results. Joseph Stalin believed that the only real power comes from a long rifle. He was dead wrong. The real power comes from within. As Alice Walker says, "The most common way people give up their power is by thinking they don't have any."

What is limiting your power? It's those sneaky little thoughts that act like anchors holding you back from your true potential. These beliefs can stem from societal or familial expectations, past experiences, and fears. Thoughts like, "I'm not good enough," "I'm too old or young for this," "I don't have the resources," "I'm just not lucky," "I'm a failure," and/or "I can't change," are familiar beliefs that limit one's progress. Do you recognize any of these? It's the stories you tell yourself that keep you from reaching for the stars.

So, how do you break free from those chains? You must identify the limiting beliefs and pay attention to that nagging voice in your head. Journaling can help you. Start by writing down the self-doubts and fears that pop up. Ask yourself where they came from and determine whether they hold you back. Next, challenge and rewire those beliefs and question their validity. Are your beliefs based on facts or just assumptions? Look for evidence that contradicts them.

Your journey to unleash your power involves confronting and conquering these limiting beliefs. Because let me tell you something, you have the power. You see, life has a way of testing you by throwing challenges and obstacles in your path. It's easy to feel overwhelmed to believe you're at the mercy of the universe and circumstances. But that's where you're mistaken. You hold the power even in a world filled with constant noise and distractions. It's crucial to remember this simple truth.

Guess what? You have the power in a world that sometimes tries to dim your light! It's crucial to remember your worth, your value, and your potential. Your past, circumstances, or limitations do not define you. Those things do not define your power. Your choices and actions determine how you show up in this world. You become unstoppable when you tap into the reservoir of strength within you and align your choices with your desires.

You become a force to be reckoned with, a beacon of inspiration for others.

As you go about your day, facing challenges and pursuing your dreams, I want you to remember these words: you have the power. Let the words echo in your mind and reverberate in your heart. Let them be a reminder that you are in control of your destiny and possess an innate ability to create the life of your dreams. As you navigate the ups and downs of life, strive for greatness, and push through adversity, always keep this truth close. You have the power, and now is the time to unleash it.

You may not realize it, but as you sit, you're beginning to tap into this inner power. It's always there—quietly waiting for you to acknowledge it. As you breathe, you sense a growing awareness of the energy that courses through your body, a sensation of strength and limitless potential. You are the master of your reality. Everything you think, believe, and act upon shapes the world around you.

You have the power to create, transform, and achieve greatness.

The power is not something external. It never was. It's an intrinsic part of who you are. Think about the moments in your life when you felt truly unstoppable. When you were able to accomplish something you once thought was impossible. Those moments are glimpses of your true power. They're proof that you are capable of greatness beyond measure. Now, imagine your life without the limitations you've placed upon yourself. Imagine a reality where dreams are not just possibilities but certainties. Feel the weight of doubt, fear, and insecurity lifting away, replaced by unwavering confidence in your abilities. And as you continue, you become more aware of your infinite power. It's like a hidden treasure waiting to be uncovered, filling you with inspiration and motivation and propelling you towards your goals.

Were you aware of this power within you? You see, the power

within you is not bound by time or circumstance. It transcends the limitations of the external world. It's a force that can shape your destiny, create your reality, and lead you to a life of purpose and fulfillment. You are becoming increasingly aware of your limitless power. It's as if a light has been switched on within you, illuminating the path to your true potential. Carry this awareness with you. Know that you possess this power to achieve whatever you desire. Embrace it, nurture it, and let it guide you to the future where possibilities are endless.

SHAPE YOUR IDEAL REALITY

This is the pinnacle of your power, the power to shape your world, which is firmly within your grasp, and it's time to unleash it to the fullest. To get started, you've got to have a crystal clear vision of what your ideal reality looks like. Envision it vividly and feel its emotions—joy, fulfillment, and excitement. Imagine every detail, from the sights to the sounds to the people you're with, visualizing with unwavering belief as if it's already happened. This visualization, faith, and emotional embodiment isn't daydreaming. It's planting the seeds of your future reality using the combined power of your subconscious mind and imagination.

Now, remember those limiting beliefs that we talked about? It's time to kick them to the curb. Believe in the extraordinary power within you. It's the power to overcome challenges, learn to adapt, grow, and know that any obstacle in your path is just a stepping stone toward your ideal reality.

Creating your ideal reality isn't just about wishful thinking. It's about taking inspired action. By taking action, you show faith in this incredible power that you have within you. Taking action is the true unleashing of your power. Break your vision down into actionable steps. What can you do today to move closer to your ideal reality? Small, consistent actions build the foundation for profound changes. The kicker is it won't always be smooth sailing. Life has its curveballs and distractions that can pull you off course. If you remind yourself that you have the power, it doesn't matter how many distractions come into play. You have the power to stay focused and overcome any challenge when you surround yourself with positive influences and keep moving forward, even when the going gets tough.

If you're unaware you have this power, nothing else matters. So, if I could just repeat over and over again, "You have the power," it would be enough. By saying, "I have the power," and recognizing that you can change your beliefs, you're almost all the way there. Above all else, I want you to remember that the power to create reality is within you. It's a force waiting to be unleashed, and the potential available to you is limitless. Go ahead, step into your power. Visualize your ideal reality. Believe in yourself, take inspired action, and stay committed. Your dreams are within reach, and the power within you to bring them to life has now been activated.

Let's do a quick visualization to amplify your power to unleash your power. As you settle into deep relaxation, become aware of your breath. Inhale slowly and deeply and exhale fully, releasing tension or stress with each breath. With each breath, let go of the external world and turn your attention inward to the boundless reservoir of power within you. Imagine a brilliant, radiant light at the center of your being. This light is your inner power and unique essence and shines brightly within you as you breathe deeply and rhythmically. Visualize this inner light, expanding and filling every cell of your body. From the tips of your toes to the top of your head, view this light growing brighter and more intense with each breath. This inner light represents your limitless potential, your capacity to achieve, and your innate strength. It is the source of your resilience in the wellspring of your power. Imagine this radiant light extending beyond your body, creating a luminous aura around you. This aura is a forcefield of confidence, determination, and self-belief. It is impenetrable and shields you from doubts, fears, and external influences. With your inner light glowing brilliantly in the aura surrounding you, take a moment to connect with your deepest desires and intentions. See them clearly in your mind's eye as if they have already become your reality.

AFFIRMATIONS—UNLEASH YOUR POWER

Now feel the power of your intentions resonating with the radiant light within you, and know that you can manifest these desires into your life.

As you continue to breathe silently, repeat these affirmations:

- I am connected to my inner power.

- I trust my limitless power.

- I am the architect of my destiny, and I have the power to shape my life in remarkable ways.

- Every challenge I face is an opportunity to tap into my inner strength and unlock my full potential.

- I know the immense power within me, and I now choose to harness it for my highest good.

- The power of my subconscious mind is a wellspring of

creativity and transformation, and I use it wisely to manifest my desires.

- I release any limiting beliefs that have held me back and embrace the infinite power of my mind to achieve my goals.

- My thoughts are charged with dynamic power, and I attract positive outcomes into my life.

- If I am in tune with the healing power of my mind, I use it to promote physical and emotional well-being.

- Every day, I affirm my inner power and allow it to guide me toward success, happiness, and abundance.

- The power of my mind is limitless, and I tap into it to overcome challenges and achieve my dreams.

- I radiate confidence and inner strength, knowing that the power within me is greater than any external circumstance.

- I am grateful for the boundless power within me, and I unleash it to create a life of purpose and fulfillment.

- I AM the source of my power.

- My power increases easily and quickly in the best interest of all.

Now is the time for you to unleash this power. Remember that you can access this wellspring of power within you whenever you choose. Carry this sense of empowerment with you as you open your eyes and return to your day, knowing you can achieve anything you want and set your mind to.

You are powerful, and your potential is boundless. Take a deep breath and slowly exhale. When you're ready, carry this sense of empowerment and inner strength throughout your day, and watch as it transforms your life so you can be Magnetic AF.

CHAPTER THREE

BE MAGNETIC AF

"You are the most powerful magnet in the universe! You contain a magnetic power within you that is more powerful than anything in this world, and this unfathomable magnetic power is emitted through your thoughts."

— *Rhonda Byrne*

In the realm of thought and emotion, there exists a power so compelling, so transformative it can only be likened to a force of nature.

This is the power of personal magnetism, and it will make you magnetic as fuck.

Your presence alone can alter the atmosphere of a room where your words not only speak to the ears but resonate with the souls of others. This is not a mere fantasy; it is the reality of those who harness the power of magnetism.

While reading the pages of this chapter, you will learn to tap into this extraordinary force and energy that lies dormant within you, waiting to be awakened. Magnetism is not just about attracting others. It is a way of being that draws in the very experiences you yearn for—deep connections, abundant prosperity, and adventures that resonate with the core of your being.

Being magnetic is not an inborn trait reserved for the few but a skill, a cultivated art that can be learned and mastered. Magnetism is about aligning your inner world with the outer, creating a harmony that resonates with authenticity and purpose. By embracing this power, you will find the world responds in kind, reflecting the energy you emit through relationships that uplift you, opportunities that inspire you, and a life rich with meaning and wonder.

MASTERING MAGNETISM

Let's explore the depths of your mind, unlock the secrets of your emotions, and learn to project a presence so compelling that the universe itself seems to conspire in your favor. A strong and stable emotional presence is the gateway to a new way of living and a path to become irresistibly magnetic in every facet of life.

Imagine you start your day with a simple walk to the local coffee shop. As you stroll with your warm smile and friendly greetings made to passers-by, their morning seems to brighten. Inside the coffee shop, you strike up a conversation with a stranger who turns out to be a local business owner. Intrigued by your insights and charm, the business owner offers a lucrative consulting gig on the spot.

Later that day, you visit a small art gallery. Your genuine interest in the artist's work and your ability to engage in thoughtful conversation impress the gallery owner. This interaction leads to an invitation to an exclusive art event where you meet several influential people, effortlessly expanding your social and professional network. In the afternoon, you decide to do some shopping and visit a boutique. Your enthusiasm and positive feedback about the products brightened the shopkeeper's day, leading to an impromptu discount and an invitation to a VIP customer event.

As the day winds down, you join a group of friends at the park. Your infectious laughter and storytelling draw others into the group, turning a casual gathering into a lively community event. People are left feeling uplifted and connected, all thanks to your natural ability to bring people together from your magnetism. People look at you and smile. You brighten up every single room.

You are magnetic, and days that unfold with endless opportunities are what I want for you. At the very core of your being lies a remarkable force, a dynamic energy that shapes your interactions, your successes, and the quality of your relationships.

This force is personal magnetism. It's more than charisma. It's an energy that emanates from within, captivating those around you and drawing towards you the very experiences you desire. It's about creating a life that is not only successful but also rich in depth and meaning.

Magnetism is akin to a magnet pole, an invisible yet undeniable and intrinsic power that makes certain individuals stand out in a crowd, effortlessly draw others to them, and seem to attract opportunities as if by magic. But here's the secret. This magnetism is not a rare gift bestowed upon a select few. It's a quality that lies within you, waiting to be unlocked and harnessed.

In relationships, magnetism plays a pivotal role. It's about more than just making a good first impression. It's about creating a lasting impact. A magnetic individual radiates warmth and sincerity that fosters deep, authentic connections, whether in personal friendships, romantic endeavors, or professional networks. Magnetism helps build bonds based on genuine understanding and mutual respect. When it comes to wealth and abundance, magnetism acts as a catalyst to attract financial success and opportunities for growth and achievement.

A magnetic mindset sees possibilities where others see obstacles, turning challenges into stepping stones toward greater success. This mindset, combined with a compelling presence, opens doors and creates opportunities that align with your goals and aspirations.

Personal magnetism helps you weave a vibrant life and attract experiences that resonate with your deepest desire and truest self, whether adventure, learning, or personal growth. A magnetic individual draws experiences that are not only fulfilling but also transformative.

The journey to becoming magnetic begins with self-awareness and involves:

- Understanding your unique strengths.

- Embracing your authenticity.

- Aligning your thoughts and actions with your deepest values.

This alignment creates an inner clarity and confidence that radiates outward, making you more approachable, relatable, and influential.

Cultivating a positive, growth-oriented mindset is essential to developing your magnetism. It involves nurturing thoughts that empower and inspire, fostering an attitude of gratitude, and maintaining a focus on solutions rather than problems. This mindset elevates your spirit and promotes those around you, creating a magnetic ripple effect.

Magnetism is a transformative power that can reshape your life and bring into your orbit the relationships, wealth, and experiences you desire and deserve. By understanding and cultivating this inner force, you open yourself to a world of possibilities. It's about becoming a beacon of positivity, a catalyst for change, and a magnet for all the good that life has to offer.

Your magnetic journey begins with a choice: embracing and unleashing the magnetic power within you. Following are a few examples of how embracing magnetic power expanded and enriched my clients' lives.

Elena, a software engineer, always felt invisible in her bustling office. Despite her talent, her quiet nature kept her in the shadows, and one day, inspired by my book, "The Reality Revolution," she contacted me. Throughout our work, she changed her posture, standing tall and confident, and began engaging more with colleagues, asking about their day with genuine interest.

Slowly, her presence in the office transformed. She told me she wasn't just noticed by her colleagues; she was appreciated, and her ideas, once hidden, were now heard and celebrated. She realized it wasn't just about being listened to; it was about the energy she brought into a room. Her newfound magnetism had changed not only how others saw her but also how she saw herself.

My friend Marco was a struggling artist and while talented, he couldn't seem to sell his paintings. He stumbled upon the concept of personal magnetism and began applying it to his life. He started visualizing his success and speaking about his art with passion and conviction. He transformed his mindset from one of scarcity to one of abundance. Astonishingly, things in his life began to shift. His enthusiasm was the magnet that easily attracted more clients. He expanded the frequency of his exhibitions, and his art started selling. He realized that his magnetism turned him into a magnet for wealth, not just monetarily but in the richness of his experiences.

A girl named Aisha, a middle manager in a nonprofit organization, was often overlooked for promotions. After explaining to her how to become more magnetic, she implemented magnetism principles, starting with empathy and truly listening to her team's concerns and ideas. She shared her vision with a contagious passion, inspiring those around her. Gradually, her influence grew. Her team's performance improved significantly, and her superiors took notice. She was soon promoted to a leadership position. She had become a magnetic leader not by force but by fostering an environment of trust, inspiration, and shared purpose.

I have another client who craved adventure, and he explored magnetism in this same regard. He started changing his attitude, embracing his openness to new experiences, and thus became magnetic. He began attending different social events, conversing with strangers, and expressing his longing for adventure. To his surprise, opportunities began to appear—an unexpected travel buddy, an invitation to a hiking trip, and a chance to learn sailing.

His life became an exciting series of adventures, all because he became a magnet for new experiences by simply opening up to the possibilities around him.

If you research this, you will find scientific underpinnings of magnetism. Several references confirm the role of charisma and magnetism in one's personal essence.

- Research by Antonakis in 2012 in the Academy of Management Review highlights that charisma is partially innate but can be developed. Charismatic leaders are found to engage followers through emotional and value-based appeals, impacting their sense of identity and self-worth.

  > "...charismatic leaders have potent effects on followers because of their transcendental ideals and authority that facilitate the followers' identification with the leader. In those conditions, trust is solidified as psychological exchanges occur. This commitment and trust is further augmented by inspirational leadership. The inspirational leader is persuasive, and he or she encourages followers to invest in and make sacrifices toward the identified ideals, gives followers a sense of purpose, and creates meaning for actions distinct from the charismatic appeal.[5]

- Adrian Furnham and Tomas Chamorro-Premuzic, in their 2010 book, "The Psychology of Personal Selection," suggest that magnetic individuals display a blend of

---

[5] https://www.researchgate.net/publication/258221547_Transformational_and_Charismatic_Leadership

extraversion, self-confidence, and a strong sense of unique value.

- Brandon Goleman, in "Emotional Intelligence: The One Important Social Skill To Lead A Better Life, Build Happier and Meaningful Relationships, Enjoy Crazy Success At Work and Discover Why It Can Matter More Than IQ," argues that emotional intelligence is a key component of affecting social interaction, noting that empathy and the ability to regulate emotions are magnetic.

- Lynn McTaggart is a fantastic author I had the wonderful opportunity to interview. In her book, "The Field: The Quest for the Secret Force of the Universe," she discusses the concept of a human energy field or aura, suggesting that individuals can emit and perceive subtle energies.

- In Dean Radan's book, "The Conscious Universe: The Scientific Truth of Psychic Phenomena," He presents experimental evidence for the existence of psychic phenomena implying a spiritual aspect to human interactions that can be linked to magnetism.

- In "Wherever You Go, There You Are," Jon Kabat-Zinn emphasizes mindfulness's role in enhancing presence and personal impact, implying that it contributes to magnetic qualities.

FAITH AND BELIEF

To become magnetic involves cultivating faith, focusing your thoughts, speaking life, practicing gratitude generously, maintaining inner peace, and embodying love. By embracing these teachings, you transform not only your life but also the lives of those around you, creating a world of abundance, harmony, and joy.

We've discussed many authors who have given profound teachings on magnetism. Anthony Norville emphasized the power of visualization and creating a magnetic personality. He believed that by vividly imagining our desires, we attract them into our reality. He suggested that the mind is a magnet and draws whatever corresponds to its ruling state. Visualization is an active process of mentally constructing the life you aspire to lead, setting the foundation for its manifestation.

Neville Goddard's concept of living in the end is a cornerstone of understanding magnetism. He taught that to attract your desires, you must assume the feeling of the wish fulfilled. This means living and acting as if your desires are already a reality. This practice of living in the wish fulfilled aligns your energy with your goals, making you magnetic to your desires.

Both Norville and Goddard, along with other contemporary thinkers, stressed the importance of belief. The belief that you are deserving of your desires and that they are attainable is crucial in the process of magnetism and attraction. Belief isn't just cognitive; it is a deep-seated conviction that permeates your thoughts and actions, thereby magnetizing you to your goals.

Emotions are the language of the universe and the fuel for your magnetic power. Joy, love, and gratitude are particularly potent in making you as magnetic as possible. These emotions elevate your vibrational frequency, aligning you with the positive experiences and relationships you seek.

To harness the full power of magnetism, you must first identify limiting beliefs and overcome them. Often, these limiting beliefs are demagnetizing you. These are often subconscious and can sabotage your effort to attract what you desire. By recognizing and reframing your beliefs, you open yourself to a world of possibilities. When you are truly magnetic, you experience synchronicity and flow in your life.

Events and opportunities seem to align perfectly with your needs and desires. This is not mere coincidence; it is the universe responding to your magnetic energy. It is important to use the power of magnetism ethically. This means attracting what is in harmony with your highest good and the good of others.

True magnetism is not about manipulation or self-serving agendas. It's about creating value and positive impact. When you understand and apply these principles, you can transform your life and attract the relationships, wealth, and experiences you desire.

EASE AND TRUST

Magnetism is not just a skill. It's a way of living that aligns you with the abundant and benevolent nature of the universe. One of the keys to becoming extremely magnetic that I have found in my life is a subtle yet powerful concept: the art of not trying too hard and reducing the importance you place on your desires.

We've all seen it. The guy hits on the girl, and he tries too hard, and she's not interested. So, you have to learn to release the intense grip on your goals and the importance you place on them, which can paradoxically bring you closer to your goal and foster an aura of effortless attraction.

Often, in our eagerness to attract what we want, we create

counterproductive resistance. By placing excessive importance on our desires, we inadvertently convey a message of lack and desperation. The state of trying too hard can repel the very thing you aim to attract.

Instead, adopting a mindset of ease and trust can make you more magnetic. Reducing importance doesn't mean becoming indifferent or giving up on your goals. Rather, it's about approaching your desires with a balanced perspective. It involves acknowledging your aspirations while also understanding that your happiness and self-worth are not solely dependent on their fulfillment.

This balanced attitude emits a relaxed, confident energy that is incredibly magnetic. Detachment is often misunderstood as not caring. In reality, it is about caring but not worrying. It's about having faith that things will work out for the best, even if they don't follow the exact path you envision. This form of detachment is liberating. It allows you to pursue your goals passionately without the anxiety of over-attachment.

A key aspect of reducing importance and not trying too hard is to trust the process of life. It's about understanding that sometimes, things take time and that the universe has its timing. By counting the process, you align yourself with the flow of life, making your journey toward magnetism more harmonious and effortless.

Relaxation and enjoyment are powerful magnetic forces. When you are relaxed and enjoying the journey, you radiate positive energy that attracts people and opportunities. Naturally, this state of being is attractive because it signals to others that you are content and fulfilled in your being, which is inherently magnetic. Trying to control every aspect of how your desire will manifest can create tension and resistance. Letting go of the need to control and instead focusing on taking aligned action creates space for unexpected and often more fulfilling outcomes to emerge.

Finding the balance between taking inspired action and letting go is crucial. It involves being proactive in your endeavors while also being open to the journey unfolding in unexpected ways. This balance is the essence of true magnetism. The art of reducing importance and not trying too hard is a nuanced but powerful aspect of becoming magnetic. It involves a delicate balance of desire and detachment, action and trust, effort and ease. By mastering this art, you create a life that not only attracts your desires effortlessly but is also more enjoyable and fulfilling in the quest for a magnetic mindset. The first and foremost tool is simply positive thinking.

Start by recognizing and challenging the deep-seated beliefs that hold you back. This investigation involves introspection and honesty about the narratives you have told yourself. Learn the art of cognitive reframing, a technique for turning a negative thought pattern into a positive one. This practice doesn't mean ignoring reality but choosing to view challenges as opportunities for growth. For example, when faced with job elimination, instead of focusing on the loss of a job, the situation could be reframed as an opportunity to pursue more aligned work.

Remember, emotions are not just feelings but signals that guide you toward your needs and values. Learn to interpret and respond to these signals constructively. Transform emotions from obstacles to catalysts for change by recognizing the energy and emotions and using them to propel yourself forward.

MAGNETIC PRACTICES

Shifting from a fixed mindset where change and learning are deprioritized to a growth mindset where there are no limits to what you can achieve helps to develop resilience and, ultimately, magnetism. Understand that failure is not a setback but a stepping stone to learning and development. You will find resilience through challenges. Use affirmations as tools for self-empowerment. Affirmations can help you become magnetic by reprogramming your subconscious thoughts. Replacing negative self-talk with constructive dialogue means speaking to yourself with respect, encouragement, and belief.

Another factor to consider is that your habits affect how magnetic you are. Understanding the psychology of habit formation and how to establish habits that reinforce a positive mindset is very helpful in becoming magnetic. There are techniques for identifying and breaking patterns that undermine your magnetism.

Be very honest and clear with yourself, identifying negative habits that clearly make you less than magnetic. These can include poor eating habits, lack of self-care, and expressing anger and frustration for minor inconveniences. It is not complicated, but you will not be magnetic if you have bad breath. Break your negative habits, and there are a variety of ways that you can do that.

Magnetism is about momentum. Discover how to create and maintain momentum in your life. Use your mindset as the driving force behind your actions. Continuously nurture a magnetic mindset. It's a dynamic process of growth and refinement. It doesn't just transform your life, but it also changes the lives of those around you.

I have also found that cultivating empathy is a powerful magnifier for magnetism. Develop the ability to understand and share the feelings of others. Empathy is the bridge that connects individuals, allowing for deeper and more meaningful interactions.

Emotional resonance also applies to understanding how to resonate emotionally with others. True connection involves listening and feeling with one another, creating a shared emotional experience that fosters strong bonds and mutual understanding. Master the art of expressing your emotions in an authentic and considerate way. Doing so involves finding the right words and tone to effectively and respectfully convey your feelings. Dive into the world of nonverbal cues, understand how your body language and facial expressions, and even silence can communicate volumes about your emotional state.

I've also found that the more authentic I am, the more magnetic I am. Sometimes, that means being vulnerable. Uncover the strength in your vulnerability. Authentic emotional expression creates a magnetic pole, inviting others to engage you on the deepest level. Establish trust by being genuine and honest. This trust is the foundation of strong, lasting personal and professional friendships.

Definitely read up on Neuro-Linguistic Programming (NLP), which studies aligning your thoughts, words, and actions. One technique of NLP is modeling, which entails observing other magnetic people, watching their physical cues and body language, and modeling their behaviors.

SELF CONCEPT

The path to becoming magnetic is cultivating confidence and self-love within. It requires patience, persistence, and compassion, but the rewards are immense.

Self-confidence is more than just a feeling of assurance. It's a deep-seated belief in your abilities and worth. It's the quiet voice within that whispers, "You are capable; you are deserving." This belief doesn't shout; it doesn't need to. Confidence is a certainty that radiates from within, influencing every action and decision.

When you operate from a place of self-confidence, your interactions have a sense of ease and authenticity. It's not about proving yourself to others. It's about being secure in who you are. The security is magnetic, attracting others who respect and admire the competence that comes not from arrogance but from self-assuredness.

However, self-competence alone is not enough. It must be coupled with self-love, the second pillar of inner magnetism. Self-love is the unconditional acceptance and appreciation of yourself. It's recognizing your worth, irrespective of achievements or failures. This kind of love is nurturing. It's a gentle yet powerful force that transforms how you view yourself and, consequently, how the world views you. When you truly love yourself, you emit a deeply attractive warmth and openness. You become a beacon of positivity and acceptance, drawing others toward you and your light.

The path to greater self-confidence and self-love begins in your mind. The thoughts you entertain shape your beliefs about yourself, and you can consciously choose thoughts that affirm your worth and abilities. When you embrace all of yourself and operate from the space of self-confidence, a shift will occur; I guarantee it.

Affirmations and positive self-talk are your tools in this transformative process. They're not mere words but seeds you plant in the fertile soil of your mind that grow into the reality of self-confidence and self-love. It's important to treat yourself with the compassion and kindness that one would offer a dear friend. Self-love is nurtured through self-care and magnetic acts of self-love—whether physical, emotional, or spiritual. It is taking time for activities that nourish the soul, speaking to yourself with kindness, and forgiving yourself for past mistakes.

As these facets of yourself grow, so does your inner magnetism. People will be naturally drawn to you because you exude self-assurance and self-respect. You will inspire others through your words or actions and the energy you radiate. Magnetism creates an inviting and comforting space around you where others feel seen and appreciated.

A life lived with inner magnetism is not just about attracting what you desire but also a life of deep fulfillment, joy, and service. It's a life where your presence is a gift, not just to yourself but to the world.

NEGATIVE SELF-FULFILLING PROPHECY

Unseen barriers often impede magnetism. One such barrier is negative self-talk. The dialogue you have with your shelf shapes your self-perception and, by extension, how others perceive you. Constantly criticizing or doubting yourself creates a self-fulfilling prophecy, where you start to embody these negative beliefs.

A major obstacle that I have noticed is a lack of authenticity. In a world where there is often pressure to conform, staying true to yourself can be challenging. Authenticity is magnetic; people are naturally drawn to genuine and honest people. Pretending to be someone you're not or hiding your true thoughts and feelings creates an invisible barrier between you and others.

I know because I've done it. I have been inauthentic. And when I am, I lose my magnetism every time. This lack of authenticity can be felt, even if not explicitly recognized, it can deter the relationships and opportunities you seek.

Fear of failure is another anti-magnetizer. It's a major deterrent; the fear of not succeeding or, worse, the fear of how others will perceive your failures can be so paralyzing that it can prevent you from taking risks necessary for growth and achieving your goals. This fear can manifest in playing it safe or not taking any action at all, which can stifle your development and dampen your magnetic energy.

Living in the past or worrying excessively about the future can also hinder your magnetism. When you're not fully present, you cannot engage authentically with others or your current situation. Being preoccupied with past regrets or future anxieties takes away the power of the present moment, which is where true magnetism lies. This lack of presence is often palpable and can create a disconnect in your interactions and endeavors.

Resistance to change is another barrier. Change is the only constant in life, and your ability to adapt and embrace new situations is a testament to your strength and flexibility. You resist change by holding on to outdated beliefs or methods that can make you seem rigid and unapproachable, qualities that are the antithesis of magnetism.

Neglecting self-care can deplete your magnetic energy. Personal magnetism is nurtured when you're physically, mentally, and emotionally well. So, neglecting your health, be it through poor diet, lack of exercise, insufficient rest, or ignoring your mental and emotional needs, can leave you drained and unable to radiate the magnetic energy needed to attract your desires.

By addressing these barriers, you cleared the path for your natural magnetism to shine by attracting the relationships, opportunities, and experiences that align with your highest self.

KEYS TO ATTRACTING A RELATIONSHIP

A quest to attract and maintain a meaningful relationship is a universal desire. It's deeply rooted in your human experience. It's a pursuit that requires not just a desire to connect but also the understanding and application of certain principles that foster deep, lasting connections.

One of the foundational aspects of attracting meaningful relationships is listening, which is more than a passive activity. It's an active engagement when you listen attentively. You validate the other person's feelings and perspectives and create a space where they feel understood and valued. This level of understanding is magnetic; it draws people closer and deepens the bond between you.

Another key is open and honest communication. This doesn't mean just expressing your thoughts and feelings clearly but doing so with respect and sensitivity. Effective communication can resolve conflicts, clarify misunderstandings, and strengthen bonds. It requires a balance of expressing your own needs and desires while being receptive to the other person's needs and desires.

Another component is personal growth. When you're committed to your personal development, you bring more to your relationships; you become more interesting, more confident, and more engaging, all of which are qualities that attract others.

WEALTH AND PROSPERITY

Moreover, as you grow, you become better equipped to contribute positively to the growth of your relationships. Magnetism with relationships, health, and wealth is all the same. The foundation of financial magnetism lies in the power of your mind as well.

Your thoughts and beliefs about money shape your financial reality. To attract wealth, you must cultivate a mindset that is receptive to prosperity. Act as if the wealth has already been attained. This does not mean living beyond your means but adopting the habits and mindset of a financially successful person.

How would you make decisions if you were wealthy now? What would your daily habits be? How would you manage your resources? Acting as if you're already prosperous aligns your energy with that of wealth and magnetizes it to you. Developing an attitude of abundance is essential to becoming a magnet for wealth.

An abundance mindset sees limitless possibilities and opportunities for growth and prosperity. It focuses on what can be gained rather than what might be lost. Cultivate gratitude for what you already have, and be open to receiving more. This attitude radiates positive energy, and it attracts similar energy and returns. Networking and building relationships play a role in magnetizing financial success as well. Wealth often comes through connections and opportunities presented by others.

Cultivating a network of positive, success-oriented individuals helps magnetize financial success. You can build your network by being genuinely interested in others, offering value, and maintaining these relationships. The energy of collaboration and mutual support is a powerful magnetizer of economic opportunities.

As James Allen said, "We do not attract what we want, but what we are."

Rumi says, "What you seek is seeking you."

Brian Tracy says, "You are a living magnet. What you attract into your life is in harmony with your dominant thoughts."

You are magnetizing your innermost thoughts; you become magnetic in every way, shape, and form to a powerful life.

As Dale Carnegie said, "The best way to become a magnetic personality is to develop a genuine interest in other people."

AFFIRMATIONS—BE MAGNETIC AF

When you are open, receptive, authentic, honest, and compassionate with other people, you create a magnetic force that attracts the good in life. Here are some affirmations that will help you become magnetic as fuck:

- I am a magnet for positive energy and opportunities.

- My presence is captivating and draws others towards me.

- I radiate confidence, charm, and charisma.

- I attract success and abundance effortlessly.

- I am influential and inspire those around me.

- My magnetism grows stronger each day.

- My energy is infectious. I uplift everyone I meet.

- I am a beacon of positivity, attracting like-minded individuals.

- I am open and receptive to new connections and opportunities.

- My charisma is my power.

- I use it to bring joy and value to others.

- I effortlessly attract the right people and circumstances for my growth and happiness.

- I am deeply connected to the magnetic energy of the universe.

- My inner magnetism grows stronger with each passing day.

- I am confident, magnetic, and full of life.

Using these keys to magnetism will help you create the life of your dreams—so much so that it'll be easy to see how amazing you are.

CHAPTER FOUR

YOU ARE AMAZING

"When you reach for the stars, you are reaching for the farthest thing out there. When you reach deep into yourself, it is the same thing, but in the opposite direction. If you reach in both directions, you will have spanned the universe."

— *Vera Nazarian*

You are amazing. You may not realize how amazing you are. Maybe in the quiet dawn of a new day, you hear a gentle whisper that stirs within the depths of your being. It's a subtle, often overlooked murmur that echoes the truths of the universe and the secrets of your true self. This voice, your voice, speaks of a journey, a path not walked by many but one destined for you.

You are amazing; it is not just a phrase. It's the unspoken reality of your existence, the essence of your being.

As you embark on this chapter of this book and your life, remember that you are a unique manifestation of the cosmos, a brilliant constellation of thoughts, emotions, and experiences.

Each breath you take is a testament to the miraculous nature of your existence. Each heartbeat has a rhythm. The dance is in tune with the universe. The world around you is not just a physical space but a canvas for your spirit. A place where your soul can paint its journey and vivid colors of experiences and emotions. You're not merely a spectator in the grand theater of life but a key performer whose role is essential and whose presence is irreplaceable.

REMEMBER

To delve deep into the mysteries of your spirit, you must explore the boundless, dormant potential within that's waiting to be awakened. This is not a transformation through remembering and realizing that you have always been and always will be amazing. To embark on this journey, you must first embrace the power of now. The present moment is a gateway to the vastness of your amazing soul and an opportunity to connect with the core of your amazing being. In the stillness of the present, you can hear the whispers of your inner wisdom, guiding you toward a life of fulfillment and joy.

Remember, the path to self-discovery is not always linear or clear. It is a winding road, filled with twists and turns, each offering lessons and insights. Embrace these experiences, for they are the building blocks of your spiritual foundation.

Open your heart and mind to the possibility that everything you need is already within you. Your fears, doubts, and insecurities are mere illusions, shadows cast by the light of your true self. You are amazing! These words are more than a cliche. It's a mirror reflecting your innermost beauty, strength, and wisdom. In the depths of your soul, you are a universe unto yourself—vast, mysterious, and full of wonder. Inhale fully and deeply before stepping forward into the journey of your amazing self. The path ahead is illuminated by the light of your amazing spirit, guiding you toward the realization that you, in all your entirety, are truly amazing.

In the unfolding story of your life, there lies a profound truth— one that whispers the interconnectedness of all things. Dance with the cosmos to understand that you're not just a part of the universe, but the universe is a part of you. Every atom within you, every beat of your heart, is a note in the grand symphony of existence. Imagine you are a vast ocean; each wave on this ocean is unique, rising and falling with its rhythm. Yet, each is inseparable from the whole. You, like these waves, are a unique expression of the universe. Your joys, sorrows, successes, and failures are all part of this magnificent cosmic dance. Recognize that the dance is not about reaching a certain destination. It is about embracing each movement, each moment of your amazing self.

In this realization, you will learn to see yourself not as a solitary being but as a vital part of a greater whole. Just as a flower cannot bloom in isolation from the soil, the sun, and the rain, your spirit cannot flourish in isolation from the universe. You are a harmonious blend of matter and spirit woven internally into the fabric of all that is. This perspective brings with it a liberating realization that you are both the creator and the observer of your reality. Your thoughts, emotions, and actions are brushstrokes on the canvas of your existence. Yet at the same time, you are the canvas, the painter, and the artist.

In this realization, there's a freedom that transcends the confines of the ego or liberation from the illusion of separation. Embrace the notion that your existence is not a solitary journey but a shared adventure; each person you encounter and each experience you have is a reflection of the universe conversing with itself. This conversation has a harmonious exchange of energy, ideas, and love. Beyond the illusion of duality, there is no separation between "good" and "bad," "right" and "wrong," "self" and "other." These are but concepts created by the mind to make sense of the world. In reality, everything is interconnected; everything is one, and every experience is a necessary part of the amazing whole.

PERCEPTION IS REALITY

As you delve deeper into your spiritual quest, you will discover that the key to your inner peace is not changing the world around you but changing your perception of it. When you view the world through the lens of interconnectedness and oneness, you realize that challenges present opportunities for growth, and setbacks offer chances to deepen your understanding of the universe. As you journey, remember that you are an integral part of this cosmic dance. Your life is a beautiful, ever-changing melody in the symphony of the universe. Dance gracefully, embrace each moment, and let the rhythm of the cosmos guide you to the realization of your magnificence.

You are not just amazing; you're an essential part of this amazing universe. Just think about the human body. The human body comprises approximately 37.2 trillion cells, each specialized for various functions.[6] The cells work in harmony to keep the body functioning properly, similar to the number of galaxies in the

---

[6] https://www.smithsonianmag.com/smart-news/there-are-372-trillion-cells-in-your-body-4941473/

universe. The human brain contains about 86 billion neurons.[7] These neurons communicate through trillions of connections or synapses, making the brain one of the most complex structures in the known universe. If you were to unravel the DNA in your body, it would stretch from the earth to the sun and back more than 600 times.[8] Despite this, about 99.5% of the DNA from two random humans is identical.[9] Over an average lifetime, the human heart beats more than 2.5 billion times, tirelessly pumping blood throughout the body.[10] The total surface area of the human lungs is approximately equal to that of the tennis court.[11] This extensive surface area is crucial for efficiently absorbing oxygen and expelling carbon dioxide. Your bones are strong ounce for ounce; some can bear more weight than steel. Your body is home to trillions of microorganisms. Microbial cells in your body outnumber human cells and play a vital role in maintaining your health. The human eye can distinguish 10 million different colors,[12] and the ear can detect 330,000 different frequencies.[13] The body is constantly renewing itself. The stomach lining regenerates every three to four days, skin cells every 35 days, and the liver every six weeks.[14] The human brain has this remarkable plasticity. It can adapt, change, and rewire itself through a person's life, which is influenced by experiences and consciousness. If you stretched all the blood vessels in your body

---

[7] https://www.livescience.com/29365-human-brain.html

[8] https://www.ancestry.com/c/dna-learning-hub/dna-facts

[9] https://www.ancestry.com/c/dna-learning-hub/dna-facts

[10] https://www.pbs.org/wgbh/nova/heart/heartfacts.html

[11] https://web.cortland.edu/biolab/111/instructors/documents/Lab2Supplement_SurfaceArea.pdf

[12] https://www.aao.org/eye-health/tips-prevention/how-humans-see-in-color

[13] https://hypertextbook.com/facts/2005/AgathaCwalina.shtml

[14] https://www.uhsa.ag/medical-trivia-the-amazing-regenerating-body/

end to end, they would circle the Earth multiple times.[15]

Your fingerprint is unique. Even identical twins have different fingerprints. You are unique as a snowflake to the whole universe. You have amazing cognitive abilities of abstract reasoning, language, problem-solving, and introspection. You experience a wide range of emotions that no other living creature does, from love and joy to sadness and empathy. You're incredibly adaptable and capable of surviving and thriving in a variety of environments—from the Arctic tundra to arid deserts. You have a human capacity for creativity within you that has led to remarkable inventions of art, literature, and technology that constantly push the boundaries of what is possible. Think of the infinite languages, cultures, traditions, and customs in our known history. Each one of them is a reflection of you. Your mind can learn and store the vast accumulated amount of knowledge.

GOD WITHIN YOU

As you journey deeper into an understanding of your true self, there is a wisdom that whispers deep within you, "You are God." This is not a statement of arrogance, and this is not sacrilege but a recognition of the Divine spark within you. A realization that the essence of the Creator resides in every fiber of your being.

- **"I have said, Ye are gods; And all of you are children of the most High."** —Psalms 82:6-7

  This is not merely a poetic metaphor but a profound truth about your inherent nature. You are more than a physical

---

[15] https://www.healthwatchmedway.com/advice-and-information/2022-09-08/did-you-know-your-blood-vessels-could-circle-earth

entity navigating through the world. You are a manifestation of the Divine and embodiment of the universal consciousness. Many cultures have pointed to this truth.

The Upanishad's sacred texts of Hindu philosophy declare, "tat tvam asi," Sanskrit: "Thou art that." The simple yet profound statement reveals that you are not separate from the Divine—you are one with it. Embrace this realization, and understand that your thoughts and beliefs shape your reality.

Just as God spoke the world into existence, your words and thoughts can manifest your desires into your life.

Jesus proclaims, "Is it not written in your law, I have said, Ye are gods?" —John 10:34 This is not blasphemy but the primary teaching of the Master himself.

Your inner world creates your outer world. You bring forth the life you desire by aligning your thoughts with the Divine essence within you.

In recognizing your divinity, you also understand that everyone else carries the same Divine spark. And seeing the Divine in others transforms your interactions, fostering compassion, understanding, and unity. With this in mind, "Love your neighbor as yourself." —Mark 12:31 becomes not just a moral directive but a recognition of the oneness of all.

Practice seeing the world through the eyes of the Divine from which you came. View every challenge as an opportunity for growth and see every setback as a lesson in disguise. In every moment, you have the power to choose thoughts that elevate and empower you. Meditate on the idea that you are the creator of your experience. Sit in stillness and feel the power of the universe coursing through you. Connect with the Divine wisdom that guides you towards your highest good. Remember, you're not striving to become Divine. You are awakening to the divinity that has always been with you. You are a co-creator with the universe, an integral part of the infinite tapestry of existence.

In this realization lies the key to freedom, joy, and fulfilling your deepest desires. As you step into this understanding, embrace the magnificence of your true self and walk confidently on the path of your Divine journey. As you embrace the truth of your Divine nature, understand that this realization is not the final destination but rather a gateway to a deeper journey within the Divine essence of your being, which is not a static state. It is an ever-evolving process of creation and experience—a continuous unfolding of your true potential.

Consider the words "I Am that I Am" —Exodus 3:14. This powerful declaration that God's name "I Am" is not just a biblical reference to the Divine. It is a mirror reflecting your essence and acknowledging that you recognize yourself as a creator. You're an active participant in the unfolding of your life story—your every thought, word, and action springs from this core identity, shaping the world around you.

Now is the time for you to consciously wield this creative power. Begin by observing your thoughts and beliefs. Are they in alignment with the reality you wish to create? If you are God, and you do not like the reality that you're in, remember that your inner conversations are shaping your outer experiences. You manifest a life resonant with joy, abundance, and peace as you align your thoughts with your Divine nature.

Ancient wisdom teaches that the outer world is a reflection of the inner self. The Bhagavad Gita states, "As is your desire, so is your will. As your will is, so is your deed. As your deed is, so is your destiny." Your life is a canvas, and your beliefs and thoughts are the brushes with which you paint. With every stroke, you create the masterpiece of your experience. In recognizing your divinity and your amazingness, you also learn to surrender to it. Surrendering does not mean giving up your power or desire to create; rather, it is an acknowledgment of the greater flow of the universe within you. Surrender is trusting that the universe, in its infinite wisdom, is working for your highest good. It is understanding that sometimes what you perceive as obstacles are stepping stones, leading you to greater growth and understanding.

Embrace the power of this moment right now. This present moment is where your creative power is most potent. In this moment, you can choose thoughts that elevate you to take action and resonate with your Divine nature. The passage, "Be still and know that I am God" —Psalms 46:10 invites you to pause, reflect, and connect with the Divine essence within you. This journey into a realization of your amazingness is one of continual growth and discovery. As you deepen your understanding of your Divine nature, you will find that your capacity for love, joy, and peace expands.

TRANSFORM DREAMS TO REALITY

Now that you've awakened to and understand the Divine essence of your being, the next step is taking powerful, decisive action. It's about harnessing that inner divinity to transform your dreams into reality. Inspired action moves you from realization to actualization and from potential to manifestation. First and foremost, understand that your beliefs shape your destiny. As you've embraced your Divine nature, let that understanding permeate every belief you hold. Remember, as you think, so shall you become. This isn't just a philosophical musing. It's a principle that can guide you into unparalleled success and fulfillment. Set your sights high. Your goal shouldn't be just about what you think you can achieve or what you should achieve. Your aspirations should be reflections of your deepest desires and your most profound dreams because you are amazing.

By aiming high, you align with the boundless nature of your true self. Your goals are not just objectives to be achieved. They are expressions of your Divine purpose. Embrace the power of decisive action. While understanding and contemplation are crucial, they must be followed by action. Each step you take, no matter how small, is a progression toward the realization of your dreams. Action is where potential meets reality and dreams become tangible. The path to your dreams is not always linear or smooth. Embrace challenges as opportunities for growth. As an amazing being, each obstacle you encounter is an invitation to deepen your resolve and hone your skills. Diamonds are amazing because they're formed under pressure. Your challenges are not barriers. They are the catalysts for your true transformation.

Develop a mindset of resilience and positivity with this understanding. Your mindset is the lens through which you view the world. Cultivate a mindset that sees possibility in every situation, a mindset that is unshaken by setbacks. A positive, resilient mindset is your shield against the trials of life, turning obstacles into stepping stones. Nurture your body, mind, and spirit. Your physical health, mental clarity, and spiritual well-being are interconnected. A healthy body supports a clear mind, and a nurtured spirit gives you the strength to pursue your goals. Invest in yourself by exercising, meditating, and feeding your soul with practices that uplift and inspire you.

Why wouldn't you? You are amazing.

Foster deep connections with others. Your journey is not a solitary one. Build relationships that are supportive, empowering, and aligned with your values. Surround yourself with people who encourage your growth and share your vision of success. Give back and contribute. True fulfillment comes not just from achieving your goals but from contributing to the greater good. Share your gifts with the world, help others, and be a force for positive change. In giving, you receive; in contributing, you find deeper meaning and satisfaction.

Now, here's a call to action. You've recognized your Divine nature. You've recognized how amazing you are. Now it's time to live it. Set bold goals, take decisive action, overcome challenges, and contribute to the world. Remember, you're not just on a journey to achieve your dreams; you're here to unleash your infinite potential.

You are amazing, and it's time to show the world how amazing you can be.

Contemplate the miraculous nature of existence. In all its complexity and beauty, the universe is not just something you live in; it is something that lives within you. You are a microcosm of the cosmos, a reflection of the stars, the oceans, and the infinite space. Within you lies a universe of possibilities waiting to be explored and expressed. Embrace the power of curiosity and wonder. Let these truths be your guide as you navigate the landscape of your life.

In the words of the poet Rainer Maria Rilke:

> "Be patient toward all that is unsolved in your heart and try to love the questions themselves, like locked rooms and like books that are now written in a very foreign tongue. Do not now seek the answers, which cannot be given you because you would not be able to live them. And the point is, to live everything. Live the questions now. Perhaps you will then gradually, without noticing it, live along some distant day into the answer."

Your curiosities are the keys that unlock new dimensions of understanding and experience. Dare to venture into the unknown. The unknown is not a realm to fear but a horizon to be explored. It is in the spaces of uncertainty and the depths of mystery that you often find the most profound insights and experiences. But the allure of the unknown draws you into new adventures and discoveries that cultivate a sense of awe and reverence for the journey. Awe and reverence are more than emotions; they are a way of being in the world. It is the recognition of the beauty, complexity, and mystery of existence.

In awe, you find a connection to something greater than yourself, a sense of unity with the cosmos. Remember, you are a conduit for the creative energy of the universe. Your thoughts, dreams, and visions are not just illusions. They are the seeds of creation, the blueprints of your reality. Nurture these seeds with the richness of your attention and watch as they blossom into manifestations of your amazing inner world. You must engage in the playful and joyous creation of your life. It is an encouragement to live in a state of perpetual wonder—aware of your amazingness—continually expanding the horizons of your imagination and experience. Let each moment be a note in the symphony of your existence, the harmonious blend of passion, creativity, and purpose.

You may say, "I'm not that amazing." Is that what you believe? Understand that faith is not passive; it is an active, dynamic force. It is the certainty of things hoped for and the evidence of things not seen. When you align your faith with your desires, you set the process of creation in motion. You're the sculptor of your reality, shaping your world through the power of this belief.

These promises are not just a call to prayer but an invitation to affirm and envision your desired reality. When you ask with faith, without a doubt in your heart, you open yourself to the amazing abundance of the universe.

In this spirit, recognize that you are a universe unto yourself—a microcosm of thoughts, emotions, and experiences that are uniquely yours. This journey that you embark upon is yours alone. As you traverse the landscape of your life, understand that each step, each choice, each triumph, and each challenge make up your amazing existence.

The beauty of your path is in its evolution. As you grow and change, so too will your journey. Embrace this change, for it is a sign of your development and expansion. Life is a journey, not a destination. Find joy in the journey itself, the process of becoming, and the experience of living fully and authentically. Let your values and beliefs guide your actions. Your moral compass, rooted in your understanding of yourself and the world, will guide you through life's challenges.

Nothing can bring you peace but your amazing self. Peace comes from living in alignment with your true self and making choices that resonate with your deepest values. Remember, the journey is yours to create. You are the architect of your destiny, the author of your life story. Embrace the majesty of your path, for it is as unique and wonderful as you are.

AFFIRMATIONS—YOU ARE AMAZING

You are amazing. Your path is a testament to the marvel that is you. Say these affirmations to affirm how amazing you are.

- I am amazing in my unique way, and I celebrate my individuality every day.

- With each breath, I remind myself that I am amazing, capable, and strong.

- I am amazing because of my ability to overcome challenges and grow stronger.

- In every challenge I face, I see an opportunity to prove just how amazing I am.

- I'm amazing, not for what I've done, but for who I am and what I aspire to be.

- Every step I take is a testament to my amazing journey and the strength within me.

- I am amazing because I dare to be authentic to myself.

- I am amazing because I contribute positively to the world in my unique way.

- I am amazing because I possess an unbreakable spirit and an unwavering will to succeed.

- The world is a better place because I am in it.

- I love sharing my amazing qualities with others.

- I am amazing because I constantly evolve, learn, and expand my horizons every day in every way.

- I am becoming more and more amazing.

- My heart is filled with gratitude because I recognize how amazing I am.

- I am amazing in my resilience, my joy, and my capacity to love and be loved.

Now that you're tuned into your god self, it's time to let go of everything that doesn't support your amazing identity.

CHAPTER FIVE

LEARN TO LET GO

"To the mind that is still, the whole universe surrenders."

— Lao Tzu

To fully activate your power, you must learn to let go. Nothing teaches us this lesson more than nature. As autumn arrives, the trees, adorned in gold and crimson, do not cling to their leaves. Instead, they let them fall gracefully, carpeting the forest floor with a tapestry of colors. This seasonal shedding is not merely an end but a profound preparation for renewal. Similarly, in life, learning to let go of what you cannot keep or control—be it grievances, past mistakes, or unmet expectations—can free you to grow and embrace new possibilities with a lighter, unburdened spirit. In this chapter I'll reveal that like the trees that stand bare against the winter sky, poised for regrowth, you too can find strength in release, making space for new life to emerge.

THE TREASURE OF THE SUBCONSCIOUS MIND

The subconscious mind is a treasure house of infinite power and wisdom, but like any treasure house, it must be tended to with care. Our minds can also hold on to the debris of yesterday, cluttering our present and barricading our future.

Why is it so important to let go of the past? The past can be a seductive siren luring us into its comforting embrace with the haunting melodies of what was. It whispers tales of bygone days—some sweet, some bitter, yet all are gone. To live in the past is to walk in a world that no longer exists—to plant our feet in the shifting sands of time that have already slipped through the hourglass.

It would help if you did not allow the past to control your present or future life. We must live in the moment in our journey through the corridors of time; we often find ourselves looking over our shoulders, fixated on the shadows of what has been.

Reality is a mirror of your inner states, thoughts, and beliefs. It is within this understanding that we find the importance of releasing the past. To let go of the past is to free yourself from an invisible burden, the colors of your world with the hues of experiences that are no longer alive. You are the creator of your destiny, and you must acknowledge that you are not your history.

INFLUENCE OF THE PAST

The past is like a worn-out garment. Familiar? Yes, but it is likely no longer a fit for the life you wish to live. The significance of shedding the weight of yesterday lies in the fact that imagination creates reality. When you are mired in the past, your imaginative powers are confined to a script that has already been played. You become like actors replaying the same tragic scene, unable to find the exit from the stage of your own making because holding on to the past is like trying to drive forward while staring in the rearview mirror. You're bound to crash into what's ahead of you because you're not looking at where you're going.

Your past can be a heavy anchor. And if you don't cut it loose, it will drag you down, preventing you from reaching the full sail of your potential. More importantly, the past is a construct of a tapestry of memories woven with threads of events that are no longer occurring. Yet you clutch them with enthusiasm as if they are the very fabric of now.

Yes, the past can be a source of wisdom. But it can also be a specter that haunts your present—a ghostly presence that stifles the breath of the new. Stuck in the past, we become like Sisyphus, eternally pushing the boulder of bygone days up the hill, only to watch it roll back down again.

We see lovers lost in the fantasy of an old romance trying to recapture the initial flame. Technologists obsess over outdated innovations. It's the entrepreneur who laments a venture that failed, the lover who mourns a romance that ended, and the dreamer who watches the ghosts of opportunities that slipped through their fingers. These individuals are living in the echoes, not the sounds of the present. These people are not present. They are time travelers stuck in a loop, a Mobius Strip of the mind. You must release the chains of bygone days.

The past, with its myriad faces, can be an unwelcome echo in the halls of your mind—a reverberation of times that have long since faded. It's critical because, in the tapestry of your existence, the past can be a stain that obscures the beauty of what's to come. It can become the default lens through which you view your present and your future. Being stuck in the past is akin to walking through a gallery of your life's artwork, only to stop at the canvases that depict scenes you wish had been painted differently.

I frequently do a considerable amount of reading at night. Occasionally, I pause and look out the window. And in that moment of relaxed attention, quite often, some long-buried negative memory pops through the trapdoor of my mind. It may be a problem that I haven't thought of for years or maybe a fairly recent hurt or resentment.

Undoubtedly, the memory arrives at my conscious level of mind with power and authority—begging me for a repeat performance. Something that hurts my feelings wants me to be saddened all over again. Someone I didn't like wants me to hate all over again. I can take 15 minutes to review the whole episode, get myself all worked up, and become emotionally involved once more with something that was forgotten and should stay forgotten.

I'm well aware, and you should be too, that old hurts and old rejections arrive at the threshold of consciousness to get out. If you take your hands off, and by that, I mean stop reviewing and rehearsing past events, you can help that negative get out of your subconscious mind. Say something like this: "Get out of my life. You have come this far. Go out into the nothingness where you belong. You have finished your act. I want you no more." Or you can say, "I freely let go of the past; I freely let go of that which yet will be. I am a now person in a now experience."

Consider the person who is stuck in the past, and I know that you have met them. Perhaps you have one person in your life who holds on to a past love, their heart entwined with memory so tightly that new love will never blossom. Or the individual who clings to an old grievance, nursing it like a dark ember that refuses to die, consuming their peace and joy.

BREAK FREE FROM THE PRISON OF THE PAST

So, how do we break the cycle? How do we let go of the past and sail towards a future bright with promise? Neville Goddard offers us several keys:

- Assuming the feeling of the wish fulfilled means letting go of the past. Imagine how it feels to be free from the chains of the past. What joy blooms in your heart? What peace unfolds when your mind dwells in the state of having already moved on?

- Practice revision. Take an event from the past that haunts you and rewrite it in your imagination. See it unfold in a way that brings peace or closure. Through this act, you're not necessarily changing the past. You are changing the impact the past holds over you and the way your imagination creates your future based on that past event. Neville Goddard claimed the past and future are all in our imagination anyway; they do not exist. So, you can let your imagination be the torch that lights the path into a new dawn.

- Picture yourself in a reality where the past has no grip on you. Feel the liberating sensation of forgiveness, not just towards others, but towards yourself. Forgive yourself for the times you have stumbled, the opportunities you missed, and the words left unsaid.

- Embrace the present, for it is the only moment that truly

belongs to you. In the present, your power is limitless, your potential untapped. In the present, you plant the seeds of your future, not with the hands of action alone but with the fertile soil of your imagination.

Your past does not define you; it is but a series of lessons. Letting go of the past is an act of profound love and freedom. It is the ultimate expression of faith in yourself and the infinite nature of your existence.

To let go of the past, you must first make a decision. A real decision means committing to achieving a result and then cutting yourself off from any other possibility—doing so often means letting go of your past. So, begin by redefining your story. Acknowledge that the past has happened. Even if you revise it, you're not denying it. You're changing your internal imaginative memory of it. But you're also not allowing past memories to pilot your future. It's about taking control and deciding your neural impact.

By deciding that you're no longer going to let the past hurt, past failures, or past disappointments control your destiny, new neural pathways are forged as imprints within your mind. Create a vision for your future that excites you and is not tied to your past. How much of your future vision is tied to overcoming the past or doing something from your past?

Create a vision of your future that excites you and has nothing to do with your past. If your future doesn't look better than your past, then what's the motivation to move forward? You have to visualize your goals with such clarity and detail that they seem within reach. Are those goals that you're visualizing based on your past? If you have a goal to get back at an old boss for what he did, make an old lover desire you by finding a new relationship, or create your vision based upon some precedent from the past, I promise you, it will not ultimately fulfill you or excite you.

Often, I find people creating visions of their future based entirely upon the past to get back at someone or to overcome something. What if you freed yourself from the past completely, and you are free to do whatever you want, and the past had nothing to do with the future you're creating?

Visualize your goals with such clarity and detail that they seem within reach. Visualize goals that have nothing to do with your past. We must always feed our minds in a healthy way—and if we provide our minds with the past, it is not very nutritious at all. Just as you feed your body with healthy food to change your health, provide your mind with inspiration, knowledge, and new experiences.

If you want to move past your old story, it's about physiology. Change your body, your posture, and your breathing, and you can change your state of mind. Much of our body, our posture, and our breathing is tied entirely to our past. So, you can begin to let go of your past by changing your physiology. When you stand tall, breathe deeply, and move with a purpose, your emotions will follow your physiology—and you'll finally be able to let go.

Model the behaviors of those who have successfully moved on from their past. How do they speak? How do they act? What do they read? Some people have had terrible, terrible things happen to them in the past. They've experienced genocide, incredible torture, and the most horrifying traumas that you can imagine. And they have been able to move on and have wonderful lives. Emulate those who are successful in releasing the past and replicate their success in your own life.

To let go of the past is to embrace the truth that life is not happening to you. It's happening FOR you in every moment. Each encounter and every challenge are an opportunity to grow stronger, to become more, and to move forward with an unstoppable momentum. You have to let go of the anchors of your past.

We have to set our sights on the horizon of possibility and steer our lives toward the future. And to achieve the vision we see ahead, it's vital that we know we deserve it.

Letting go of the past begins with forgiveness—the forgiveness of others and, critically—of yourself. Forgiveness is to give yourself peace, freedom, and a future unchained from the past. Affirm to yourself, "I release the past and dwell in the joy of the present. I am at peace."

For a moment, picture yourself as a vessel filled to the brim with the past. Now imagine a golden light, the light of awareness and understanding shining upon you. As this light grows brighter, the past overflows and spills out, leaving you empty, ready to be filled with new experiences, new joys, and new successes. You can say, "I am released from the chains of the past. I move forward with freedom and grace." Believing in these words is important, for the power lies in your belief.

I've met people who say, "I simply can't let go of my past, Brian. It's impossible." They've done hypnosis, they've done therapy. But then they start affirming something negative when they say, "I can't." Then, they begin to believe they can't.

To release the past, we must embrace the present and engage fully with life as it is now.

Take up new hobbies, forge new relationships, and set new goals. Let go of the past to affirm life. Say yes to the infinite possibilities that await you. Walk in the light of awareness, wisdom, and understanding. Let's move forward together with open hearts and minds into a bright future that beckons us all. That bright future means letting go of the past.

When you turn on the TV or look at your social media right now, you'll see all kinds of wars and hatred. Can you guess where wars and hatred are coming from? They're coming from people who are obsessed with the past. It's in politics. It's in governments. It is in histories and cultures. Imagine if we all let go of our past and decided to come together, letting go of our resentments. Life would be different if we could let go of our distortions to release the past.

FLIP THE SWITCH

You can find that truth and excitement now. Take a moment. Take a deep breath. Feel the pulse of your heart, the energy coursing through your veins. This is life. And it is happening right now. Indulge in new experiences. Let novelty flood your senses.

Why did we enjoy our childhoods so much more? It's because we had less of a past. We are indulging in a new and wonderful experience of playing. Play is not a mere distraction. It is an act of recontextualization. By embracing the new, we dilute the old; we allow the brain to form new connections AND build new neural pathways.

And what about our memories? These precious keepsakes can be transformed. Transmute the pain of the past into lessons. Use them to propel yourself into a future ripe with possibility. Remember, we are explorers, not just of the physical realm, but of the mental one. To explore, we must move. We must evolve. And evolution is not just a matter of the body but of the mind and the soul.

How do you even know the past happened? What if today is the first day of your life, and you simply woke up with all those memories?

Embracing the concept of possibility means living with an openness from the emergent to the becoming and unfolding of life. Let us unhook our tethers and push off into the vastness of now with our eyes wide open to the awe of existence. And we can only do that by letting go of the past.

INCREASE POSSIBILITIES WITH INTENT

I urge you to step into the quantum reality of possibilities, where every moment is a new birth of potentialities. To let go of the past is to embrace this quantum field where all different futures simultaneously exist until one is observed into being. We must acknowledge the past, keep it, learn from it, and then use the power of our intention to create a different experience and set our sights on a new horizon. This is done not with a mere wish or with a potent declaration of intent.

Your intention is your rudder into the vast sea of potential. With this intention, with this new horizon, you can revise the past, you can receive it, and you can tell yourself a new story. And when you do this, you permit yourself to engage in the mental rehearsal of your desired future. You can then visualize it with such intensity that the universe begins to weave it into the fabric of reality.

You must unlock the chains of the past in order to enter into this unlimited field of possibilities. Say with me, "I release the past and embrace the future." Repeat it, "I release the past and embrace the future." Let this phrase become the mantra that echoes in your mind's corridors—just being a passive observer of this process, involving your senses, enveloping your emotions, and acting as if the future you desire is already unfolding.

This is the act of faith that bridges the gap between the world of thoughts and the world of experience. The past is simply a construct of a memory trace and nothing more. It is not the grand architect of our lives. We are letting go of the past as our Declaration of Independence, our moment of stepping into the role of the creator. Let us boldly claim our right to craft a future unfettered by the past, a future that aligns with our greatest intention and highest good. That's what the tree does. When it grows, new leaves sprout, and old leaves die. It is the natural formulation of the universe.

EMOTIONAL IMPACT

Understanding that emotions create our future, we must evaluate the emotional impact of our memories. It is extremely difficult to forget anything that hits us with an emotional impact. We can forget the trivial, and we can ignore the casual. But we do not easily let go of things delivered into our minds under heavy emotions.

Emotion is the key to life. It is the law of living.

It is well established psychologically that emotion is the only thing that really affects us. We are emotional people. And emotion is the creative power of the mind, which is why organized religion has always taught the power of love.

One of the reasons why the teachings of Jesus caught on so quickly in the Roman Empire was that he was a symbol of love. He was not a symbol of war or hate. Being the symbol of love, he interested people much more than the old gods of hate and war.

Emotions are the cornerstone of life. Yesterday carries into today only through our emotions because the memory field is a field of emotional memory.

This is why you cannot remember a casual incident that happened ten years ago. But you can place a heartbreak or some equivalent unpleasantness that shook you up emotionally at that time. The remembrance of the evils of the past is a part of the nature of the mind until the mind is cleared through spiritual treatment, imagination, visualization, and specialized techniques.

Nature arranged this because it expects its creation to clear its thoughts. Man is the creation of God as the mind. You and I have not sought to clear our minds at all times. We have wanted someone else to do it for us. Through the ages, men and women have devised many ways to facilitate clearing the mind. Many paths, prayer books, prayer wheels, statues, novenas, and saviors were created for an outside source to clear one's mind when, of course, this cannot be done.

Remember that emotion binds, retains, and holds. What you do not want to remember is stored in memory by emotion and not by common sense. You can say to it, "I no longer give you the idea, any more emotional support. I declare that you have operated on me long enough. You have managed me long enough. I now ask that you convert yourself into a positive, healthy emotion."

Commanding emotion is turning fear into faith, rejection into acceptance, disease into health, hate into love, and water into wine. This can be done. You take the hurt out of life by first admitting you are hurt. You get some understanding of why you are hurt. And finally, you say,

> "I will now withdraw my need for this hurt. I no longer need to justify the present by the past. I no longer need to justify my present inadequacies merely on the basis of something that happened years or even moments ago. I am emotionally interested in the new concept. I know what I am. And I refuse to remember what I was; I am intrigued by what I can become. And I no longer need to remember the hurts that made me what I was."

Letting go of the hurt memories is tremendously important. Most people do not like what they are. Therefore, they revert to the past rather than accept the present. When you get yourself to living this day as your own, thinking of this day, and loving living this day, you do not need to go to the past.

Jesus said:

> "No man, having put his hand to the plow and turning back, is fit for the kingdom of God. A plow moves forward, and the person behind the plow has to know where he is going; he has to know where to turn around to come back. He is so busy knowing what is to be done that he does not need to look behind him to see the furrow that he has finished." —Luke 9:62

Life is the progressive action of the now becoming the future. In order to move from here to there, I have to take up the anchors that I put down to keep me where I have been. Many people feel it is very comfortable to be anchored somewhere; the anchor drags in the past, deters them, and they find that they are not moving forward. And they do nothing about it until wisdom comes to the fore. And they pull up the anchors of the negatives holding them down. Once that's done, they are able to go full steam ahead. Having made the start, it is possible to become so fascinated with the course ahead that you completely forget about the point from which you have come.

When this happens, you can say to the hurts of yesterday, "I can't remember you except as an incident." You can tell the future, "I grasp you. I want to move forward in a creative, progressive action, propelled by a mind that is God, a life that is lived, a love that is great, and a power that responds to the good."

Accepting memories of the great experiences that brought you joy need not be erased because they are valuable, and the emotions that created them will hold them fast. Only the negative, destructive memories need to be let go unless those positive memories are holding you, where you're pining for the joys of the past so that you can't experience the joys of the present.

The past holds power as long as you feel that the past is greater than the present. As long as you nourish the past to not compete with the present, the past has enthralled you. The way to be rid of the past is to see it as experiencing growth and nothing else. We are so enmeshed in the personalities of the past and the situations of the past that we slip from the present into the past when we become past people working in the present.

The book of Isaiah was written at a time when the people were in captivity in Babylon. It was a time of great spiritual progress, even though the people were very unhappy, living not as enslaved but as a foreign minority in a distant country, and they wanted to go home.

Like most of us, these people talked about the past and the "good old days." And they kept saying to themselves, "Oh, if only things could be the way they were." They lamented, they wept, and the older gentlemen kept on saying, "Oh, if only we could have things as they were." It is then that Isaiah speaks up, saying,

- **"Remember ye, not the former things, neither consider the things of old; Behold, I will do a new thing. Now it shall spring forth, shall you not know it?"** —Isaiah 48:18-19

If your attention is so fixed upon the old patterns, the old habits, the things that used to be, and that people used to be, then you will not even see the new things I make.

What Isaiah said hundreds of years ago applies equally well to us today: you and I are the people of that which shall be, not the people of that which has been.

RELEASING THE ENERGY OF EMOTION

If you let a dead body sit in the basement, it will start to smell, so you have to get rid of it. Sometimes, people simply can't forget about the past without bringing it up, acknowledging it, and then letting it go.

Recapitulation, a technique originally developed by Toltec Shamans and later popularized by Carlos Castaneda, involves actually pulling up the memory of past experiences, evaluating it from multiple perspectives, seeing it as if in a movie theater or as an observer, vividly experiencing it, and then limiting it, shrinking it, making it black and white, and then revising it. The shaman goes through a simple process; you release those past experiences tied to emotions while removing the emotion from the energy body.

While many struggle with pulling up the original memory, I have found this to be the most effective technique. In this chapter, we have discussed numerous ways to let go of and reshape your past. Try at least one of these methods and let the leaves fall! Oh, and clean out your basement.

AFFIRMATIONS—LEARN TO LET GO

Saying these affirmations out loud will start the process of reprogramming your subconscious mind to release the past. Whenever you have the past come up, say these affirmations and remember them. Perhaps one of these makes your heart sing. If so, remember it and say it out loud when the past seems to be affecting your present.

- I release the past with ease and trust in the process of life.

- I am willing to forgive myself and others for releasing me from the chains of the past.

- I choose to let go.

- Old, negative patterns no longer limit me. I let them go with love.

- Each moment is a new beginning.

- I let go of fear and pain.

- I live in love, and my heart is open.

- I allow myself to feel the fullness of joy and the possibility of a positive future.

- I lovingly release all things that no longer serve me.

- I trust my journey.

- My future is bright and filled with joy.

- I am at peace with what was, what is, and what will be worthy of a future shaped by love.

- As I let go of the past, I make room for new love and happiness to enter my life.

- Anew, I am supported in my healing journey.

- The past has no power over me. With every breath, I release the anxiety and anger of what has been and welcome peace and love into my heart.

Go out into the day in the now, enjoying the now, letting go of the past, and creating a bright new future. You are the architect, and never forget—your future is brighter when the past does not cloud it.

In addition to letting go of the past, claiming your bright future requires dismantling the distortions that keep you from seeing situations clearly.

CHAPTER SIX

GET FREE FROM DISTORTIONS

"We must not confuse distortion with innovation; distortion is useless change, art is beneficial change."

— *Chuck Jones*

I've had a wonderful opportunity to work with many people trying to fulfill their desires to overcome obstacles. One common element that is a little prickly to overcome is cognitive distortions. When I teach that thought creates reality, it then becomes important to assess what you are thinking and what you are believing. We have full access to God's power with one condition. And that is, "Do we believe?" But, our beliefs are often shaded by these cognitive distortions that undermine an understanding of who we are and the world around us. These distortions take us away from the truth and send us down rabbit holes that lead to nowhere—literally nowhere.

These cognitive distortions are so prevalent, particularly when reading social media, especially in politics, that they are used to manipulate in various ways. Distortions are a part of the programming that locks you into your current reality, and we'll explore 12 common distortions in this chapter.

For us to take advantage of our ability to create our reality, we must dissolve and dismantle the cognitive distortions in our lives. A distorted thought or cognitive distortion—and there are many— is an exaggerated pattern of thoughts that are not based on facts, leading people to more negative perspectives. Cognitive distortions are the mind's way of making you believe things that aren't necessarily true. Particularly, when you process these distortions as facts, the impact can be major. The way you show up, behave, and impact based on faulty assumptions can keep you on the wrong side of the reality you want.

Everyone falls into cognitive distortions on occasion. It's a part of the human experience. This particularly happens when you're not feeling your best. But, consistently engaging in negative thoughts can negatively impact your mental health—especially when these thoughts become things.

Cognitive distortions create timelines and realities where catastrophes, sickness, and terrible accidents can occur because you are locked into these negative thoughts. You can learn to identify cognitive distortions to know when your mind is playing tricks on you so you can reframe and redirect them quickly so they don't negatively impact your mood, behaviors, and reality.

Cognitive distortions are biased ways of thinking that cloud our judgment, warp our perception, and often lead to negative emotions and unhealthy behaviors. Understanding these distortions is crucial, as it sets the foundation for positive change and personal growth. Cognitive distortions are not just abstract psychological concepts. They are lived realities that shape your everyday experience. These distorted thinking patterns are like lenses that alter how you see yourself and others in the world around you. Distortions turn minor setbacks into insurmountable obstacles, fleeting thoughts into fixed beliefs, and manageable situations into overwhelming crises. The influence of cognitive distortions cannot be overstated. They can hold you back, limit your potential, and keep you trapped in a cycle of negative thinking and self-doubt—distorting your perceptions and leading you to interpret situations in ways that reinforce your deepest insecurities and fears.

IMPACT OF COGNITIVE DISTORTIONS

Why do you fall into these patterns of distorted thinking? Often, cognitive distortions are rooted in past experiences, trauma, or learned behaviors. They are the mind's way of coping with stress and uncertainty. However, while they may provide temporary relief or a sense of control, these distortions do more harm than good in the long run.

The good news is that you have the power to change these patterns.

I once worked with a girl named Sarah. She was bright and ambitious, with dreams and potentials clouded by the deceptive power of her distorted thinking. She had always been a top performer academically and in her burgeoning career. She was known for her diligence, attention to detail, and unwavering commitment to excellence. However, like all of us, Sarah was not immune to the occasional bouts of self-doubt and negative thinking. So, one fateful day, she was assigned a high-profile project at work, something she had been manifesting and eagerly anticipating for months. This opportunity was her chance to shine, prove her worth, and take a significant step forward in her career. However, as the deadline approached and the pressure began to mount, she found herself entangled in a web of cognitive distortions.

She started filtering out all the past successes, focusing solely on the times when she previously failed. And then she had relentless thoughts: "I'm not good enough for this," "I've never been able to do this," "I'm going to mess this up." These incessant thoughts became her constant companions. She overgeneralized every minor setback, interpreting them as evidence of her perceived incompetence. She looked at everything as proof that she couldn't do it, and she began catastrophizing the situation, convincing herself that failing this project would ruin her career and tarnish her reputation irreparably.

She discounted all the positive feedback she received in the past, allowing the negative thoughts to overshadow her accomplishments. This vortex of distorted thinking left her paralyzed by fear and self-doubt. She withdrew from her colleagues and was not able to complete the project. Because she catastrophized, she did not advance in her career and was demoted. After I talked for a little bit with her, it appeared that she could have completed the project very easily, but she let her negative thoughts cloud her judgment. Her distortions directly impacted her ability to complete this ever-important project, which, if she had completed it, would have springboarded her into different places in her company. With a successful project under her belt, she definitely would have moved up, which also would have helped her mentally.

I see this all the time with people who use affirmations. They'll say the affirmation, and then when thinking about the words they are saying or talking about the affirmations with me, they will say, "Well, it's not true." And they'll mention these distortions as justification. So, I wanted to go over 12 common cognitive distortions. Remember, there are many more than this, but these are patterns of thought that reinforce your negative beliefs and keep you trapped in a cycle of negative thinking and emotional turmoil. It's impossible to live the life of your dreams when negative beliefs and emotions are running the show.

FILTERING

The 1st distortion I see all the time, and I'm very guilty of, is filtering. Filtering is a cognitive distortion where we focus solely on the negative aspects of a situation, ignoring any positive elements. It's like looking through a lens that only highlights the bad, making it difficult to see the good. For example, if you receive positive feedback at work and a small piece of constructive criticism, you might fixate on the criticism and disregard the praise. I do this all the time. When I have a video I'm excited about, I'll review the comments. Typically, the comments are wonderful, and everybody's being so complimentary. If one person says something terrible, like "I hate your voice," "You talk too fast," or "You slurred your words," all I can think about is that one negative comment—even though 99% of the other comments were positive.

I encountered this earlier in my life when I worked at General Motors. I had a performance review, and my manager complimented me on my hard work several times, reviewing a list of glowing things they enjoyed about my work. Ultimately, they made one tiny improvement suggestion, and I left that meeting feeling miserable and dwelling on that one suggestion all day. I've seen filtering in relationships and nearly every other aspect of life. Filtering is a distorted thinking pattern where an individual focuses exclusively on negative aspects. Filtering can happen in several ways.

Selective attention, where the individual focuses on the negative details of a situation while the positive aspects are overlooked or dismissed. Another example of this is negative bias, where you've viewed situations, people, or yourself through a pessimistic lens, which can lead to feelings of sadness, anxiety, or low self-worth. This negative bias can reinforce existing negative beliefs and attitudes, creating a vicious cycle of distorted thinking and negative emotions.

Have you ever been around people and all they do is complain or point out the problems in the world? Even when the problems are real, that's all they do. They look at every politician as corrupt. They look at every salesman as manipulating. And they always look at the lowest level for everybody they meet. Another consideration is how these negative views impact your behavior. When someone consistently focuses on the negative, they may be less likely to take risks or pursue other opportunities out of fear of failure or disappointment. They may engage in avoidance behaviors and steer clear of situations that they anticipate will have negative outcomes.

POLARIZATION

The 2nd cognitive distortion is polarization, which is thinking about yourself and the world in an all-or-nothing way. A person with polarized thinking tends to categorize everything as black or white with no shades of gray. This type of cognitive distortion leads you to say your coworker was a saint until they ate your sandwich. Now, you cannot stand her. Or you earned a poor grade on your last test, so you believe you failed at being a good student. Despite only ever getting A's before, polarized thinking can create unrealistic standards for yourself and others that could affect your relationship and motivation. These black-and-white thoughts set you up for failure.

For example, if you've decided to eat healthy foods and today, you didn't have time to prepare a meal, and you eat a bacon cheeseburger, this immediately leads you to conclude that you've ruined your health routine. Further, you may decide to no longer try to get healthy and feel that nothing you do will work anymore. When you engage in this polarized thinking, everything is in either a "good" or a "bad" category, and without considering every variation between "good" and "bad," you may miss the complexity of most people and situations.

Polarization involves seeing things in extremes. Why is it when you're following the newest event on the news that you think in the extremes, like imagining that this is the end of the world? Situations are either perfect or disastrous, people are either wonderful or terrible, and outcomes are either complete successes or utter failures. This extreme thinking leaves no room for the complexity and nuance inherent in most situations and will raise thinking that can profoundly affect how individuals perceive themselves. As a result, they may set unrealistically high standards and then view themselves as failures when they inevitably fall short. This can lead to having a negative self-image and expanded feelings of low self-esteem and inadequacy.

A lot of times, politicians want you to be polarized and divided, so they speak with polaristic language. In 2022, Dominic Packer & Jay

Van Bavel completed research on how politicians use polarized language. They note the impact of such language, stating, "Polarizing language can be effective in influencing people's attitudes and behaviors—mobilizing supporters and swaying opinions. For example, framing an issue in terms of what your group could lose and what another group could gain coupled with words like "fascist, "enemy," and "horror" can influence people to adopt a more extreme viewpoint."[16]

Polarization reflects a form of rigid thinking, where the individual is stuck in their extreme viewpoints and unable to see alternative perspectives. This rigidity can claim one's ability to problem solve, adapt to change, and navigate life's complexities. What I find fascinating is that I'll come upon somebody who has this cognitive distortion of polarization. And then when you mention, "Hey, I think it would be really good if you overcome this polarization." They'll say, "Yeah, everybody is so rigid in their thinking." And when we delve deeper, it's clear to see they believe everybody else in the world is wrong, they're right, and they're always right. Of course, that means everyone *else* needs to learn how to think properly.

Not surprisingly, polarization can affect relationships and lead to unrealistic expectations and misunderstandings. If an individual views others in extreme terms, they may have difficulty seeing the good in people when they make mistakes or behave in less-than-ideal ways. This view can strain relationships and contribute to conflict and disconnection. Overcoming polarization involves cognitive restructuring, where you learn to recognize and challenge your polarized thoughts. You can practice viewing situations and people on a continuum rather than in absolute

---

[16] https://powerofus.substack.com/p/how-politicians-leverage-polarizing

terms. Everything doesn't have to be dualistic. For example, instead of thinking of a work project as a complete success or failure, you might evaluate specific aspects of the project to identify what portions went well and what could be improved.

Part of challenging polarization is learning to embrace ambiguity and uncertainty. Life is rarely black and white, and learning to tolerate the gray areas can lead to greater flexibility, resilience, and well-being. One way to combat polarization is to adopt graded language. Instead of using absolute terms like "always" or "never," individuals can use more nuanced language such as "sometimes" or "partially." This shift in language can reflect a more balanced and realistic perspective.

Polarization can lead to intense emotional highs and lows as individuals swing between viewing situations in extremely positive or negative terms. Challenging this distortion can cultivate a more stable and balanced emotional state. Overcoming this polarization is crucial for building resilience. Life is full of ups and downs, and viewing setbacks as temporary and specific rather than complete failures can contribute to greater perseverance and a sense of agency.

OVERGENERALIZATION

The 3rd major cognitive distortion is overgeneralization. Overgeneralizing occurs when an isolated negative event is generalized into a repeating negative pattern. With overgeneralization, words like "always," "never," "anything," "nothing," or "frequent" are in your train of thought. So, you see one person do one bad thing. Maybe this person is Dutch, and then you say, "Well, all Dutch people are bad." Not all overgeneralizations are as obvious as that. Another example is speaking up in a meeting, not having your suggestions included, and then generalizing the meeting's outcome by thinking, "I never say the right things. They'll never want to promote me."

When you're thinking with overgeneralized words like "always," "never," "anything," "nothing," or "frequent" in your train of thought, they can manifest in your thoughts about the world and its events. When you're running late for work and on your way there, you hit a red light that makes you late, you think, "Nothing ever goes my way," and then you see nothing ever going your way.

Overgeneralization is incredibly important to understand. Oftentimes, you'll see people making broad, sweeping conclusions based on a single event or a piece of evidence. We must stop doing this. This distorted thought process can significantly affect our perception of ourselves, others, and the world around us. Overgeneralization involves drawing broad conclusions from a single or limited number of events. Overgeneralization can lead to negative self-image and low self-esteem. When individuals view their mistakes or setbacks as indicative of their overall worth or abilities, they may develop a harsh, critical view of themselves. This distortion can lead to negative feedback loops where the initial overgeneralization leads to negative emotions, which in turn reinforces the distorted thinking pattern. This cycle can be difficult to break without intervention.

Overgeneralization can also occur across different domains of one's life. For example, a person might have a negative experience in a social setting and conclude that they are socially inept in all situations. In relationships, overgeneralization can lead to misunderstandings and conflict. If you believe a friend's single act of thoughtlessness means they are always inconsiderate and thoughtless, it can strain the relationship, or you can lose a good friend who made a single mistake. Maybe you're in a relationship, and your partner makes a single mistake, and then you generalize that this person is going to do this forever, and you break up with them when you are perfect for each other, but you generalize that one event into something much, much worse.

Part of cognitive restructuring involves seeking evidence to challenge the overgeneralized belief. This can involve reflecting on past experiences to find counterexamples to disprove the sweeping conclusion. As a strategy, overgeneralization is very similar to catastrophic thinking, where you're always looking for the worst possible outcome.

JUMPING TO CONCLUSIONS

The 4th cognitive distortion I see all the time is jumping to conclusions. Jumping to conclusions happens when you negatively interpret an event or situation without proper evidence to support your decision. For example, if your partner looks serious when they come home after a long day, you may conclude that they're mad at you and keep your distance instead of engaging with curiosity and asking how their day was. It's highly possible your partner just had a rough day at work, and whatever they're serious about has nothing to do with you.

Jumping to conclusions or mind-reading is often a response to a persistent thought pattern. It may have nothing to do with what another is thinking. I see it all the time. People think they know what others are thinking when they have no idea. After a conversation, someone might think, "She didn't smile much. She must think I'm boring," despite having no concrete proof of the other person's thoughts. Then, slowly, over time, they let this thought fester and consistently believe the other person thinks they're boring.

Or an employee might believe, "My boss didn't greet me this morning. He must have been upset with me," without any additional information about the boss's mood or thoughts. Jumping to conclusions can produce negative emotions, strain relationships, and create misunderstandings because the assumptions are often inaccurate. You may be torturing yourself over something because you've jumped to the conclusion when, in fact, your assumption is not true.

Another aspect of jumping to conclusions is fortune telling, which predicts a negative outcome for a future event, often leading to worry and anxiety. Before a test, you might say, "I'm going to fail despite being very well prepared," or someone waiting for a medical test might assume the results are going to be bad, something is seriously wrong, and they worry about it, making themselves sick. This kind of thinking can cause major anxiety while preventing you from taking risks or trying new things. Unfortunately, these negative expectations can create a self-fulfilling prophecy, where the negative expectation influences your behavior in a way that makes the negative outcome more likely.

Before jumping to a conclusion, ask yourself, "What is the evidence for and against my thoughts?" This approach can help create a more balanced view of the situation. Consider other possible explanations or viewpoints. For example, if you think your friend is ignoring your text because they're mad at you, consider that they might just be busy and haven't seen the message yet. Ask yourself, "What's the likelihood that what I'm worried about will happen?" and "Has it happened before?" Exploring these questions can help put things in perspective.

Practice staying in the present moment rather than getting lost in future possibilities or assumptions about others' thoughts.

Mindfulness and staying present can be very helpful if you tend to jump to conclusions. Sometimes, discussing your thoughts and gaining an outside perspective can help challenge your conclusions. Trusted friends, family members, and therapists can help you grow beyond this distortion. And if you have friends you trust willing to tell you when you're wrong, they'll let you know when you're jumping to conclusions. Remind yourself that everyone makes mistakes, and the negative outcomes do not necessarily reflect your worth or abilities. By actively challenging and reframing thoughts associated with jumping to conclusions, you can develop a more balanced, rational way of thinking, leading to improved emotional well-being and healthier relationships.

CATASTROPHIZING

The 5th common cognitive distortion is catastrophizing. Related to jumping to conclusions, catastrophizing happens when you imagine the worst possible outcome, even when it's improbable or unlikely. This cognitive distortion often comes with what-if questions. "What if he didn't call because he got into an accident?" "What if she hadn't arrived because she didn't want to spend time with me?" "What if I help this person, and they betray or abandon me?"

I saw this distortion with my mother all the time, and it was rather frightening. She would say, "You've got to be careful," "There are murderers out there," or my favorite is that she would say, "Be careful driving home." I was driving home from Kansas to Colorado once, and she'd say, "You got to be careful with the black ice. There's just so much black ice out there." I checked the weather and the news, and there were no reports of black ice anywhere on the long stretch of highway I had to drive. But halfway through my drive, I noticed I started slipping. Black ice is something you cannot see. Sure enough, I encountered black ice on my drive. I am guaranteeing that her catastrophizing of this event created that situation.

Catastrophizing is a very powerful manipulative device. People will use it to manipulate you; they will tell you the worst possible event and then say, "Oh, I have a solution for that," or "I have a way of overcoming this." So be very careful when people over-catastrophize when they are telling you the worst possible event that can happen. Maybe you see somebody who has mild pain in their chest, and they immediately think, "I'm having a heart attack, and I'm going to die," instead of considering more benign possibilities. I see it in health all the time. Or an employee makes a minor mistake on a report and assumes he will be fired without any indication that would be the case. This form of catastrophizing, predictive catastrophizing, can cause intense anxiety, can prevent individuals from taking action due to fear of the perceived impending disaster, and can lead to avoidance behaviors.

Another example of this is magnification catastrophizing. This distortion involves magnifying the significance or implications of an event, perceiving it as far more significant or harmful than it is. For example, after a social gathering, a person obsesses over a small awkward moment, thinking, "Everyone noticed, and now they all think I'm weird and incompetent." Or a student gets a lower grade than expected on an assignment and thinks, "This is it. I'm going to fail the course and ruin my entire academic career.

I will never be able to finish my degree, I won't be employed, and all is lost." Magnification catastrophizing can lead to overwhelming emotions, distorted perception of events, and heightened distress.

Challenge your catastrophic thoughts by asking yourself:

- What is the evidence for and against my thought?

- What's the worst that could happen?

- How likely is it?

Divide the situation into smaller parts to assess which aspects are realistic concerns and which are exaggerated. Again, practice staying in the present moment and using grounding techniques. Think about the situation and consider the following: the best possible outcome, the most likely outcome, and the worst possible outcome to gain a balanced perspective. Create and use coping statements such as "I can handle uncertainty, where I've dealt with similar situations before." If catastrophizing is leading to avoidance, this is important. Consider using a graded approach to gradually face and cope with a feared situation.

Suppose catastrophizing is significantly impacting your quality of life. In that case, you should get help, you should meditate, and you need to do something about it because it is one of the first steps that can lead to depression, sadness, and mental health problems.

THE FALLACY OF FAIRNESS

The 6th distortion is the fallacy of fairness. We all tend to view the world as fair and measure each experience and behavior on an internal fairness scale. When we find that others have a different value for what's fair and it doesn't align with our values, we can be resentful. This fallacy can make you think you know what's fair and what isn't. Being on opposing sides of fairness can lead to conflicts because you're fighting for your version of fairness, which is often self-serving. For example, when your partner comes home after a long day to a scrumptious meal you cooked, it may seem fair that they reciprocate by finishing the laundry. However, they arrive home exhausted and want to read a book instead of doing the laundry. They believe it's fair to carve out some downtime after a busy day so they can be present with you for the rest of the evening.

Considering individual needs or circumstances, it is wrong to believe everyone should be treated equally in all situations. For example, say I work just as hard as my coworker. It's only fair that we get the same recognition and rewards. That's just not how the world works. Holding on to anger or resentment when situations do not seem fair can work against you. You could say, "I always help my friends when they need it, but they weren't there for me when I needed it. It's just not fair." Creating strict internal rules about how people should behave and getting upset when those rules are not followed can work against you. I've seen people, particularly at the beginning of a relationship, get super angry about something their partner does or says because they have this unwritten rule about fairness. They may claim that their partner is not respecting their needs and that what they did was not right. Meanwhile, their partner is not even aware of the internal rules about how people should behave. Of course, this ends up working against them, and the relationship fails—when it was a great relationship, and it was just the cognitive distortion about the fallacy of fairness getting in the way of their success.

You can employ a few strategies to combat the fallacy of fairness.

- Ask yourself if your definition of fairness is realistic, and consider whether flexibility is beneficial.

- Try to understand situations from others' perspectives, practice empathy, and consider their needs and circumstances.

- Acknowledge that life is inherently unfair sometimes, and focus on how you can respond constructively rather than dwelling on injustices done to you.

- Understand and communicate your limits effectively rather than expecting others to inherently know what is fair.

- In relationships and interactions, strive for compromise and mutual understanding instead of rigid rules of fairness that you apply to a situation.

- Shift your focus from what seems unfair to what you're grateful for.

- Holding on to feelings of resentment harms you more than others. Practice letting go and moving forward.

BLAMING

The 7th common cognitive distortion is blaming. People love to blame others, events, and other things for their problems, and this action creates a distortion that is very significant and affects you dramatically. Blaming refers to making others responsible for how you feel. Saying, "You made me feel bad," usually defines this cognitive distortion, and it comes with the belief that others have the power to impact your life. However, even when others engage in hurtful behaviors, you still control how you feel in most situations. For instance, if you're upset most of the day after your partner made a comment about your new dress while you were getting ready, you're blaming. If you're thinking, "My partner made me feel bad about myself when he said he didn't like my dress," that's not true because you are in control of how you feel. Are you aware of this? You are responsible for everything that happens in your life within your sphere of influence. There's no need to blame anyone else.

This distortion leads to a lack of accountability. It strains relationships, hinders personal growth, and places blame on others for one's feelings, actions, or misfortunes, and it is wrong. I've heard someone say, "It's my team's fault that I didn't finish the project on time. They didn't support me enough, so it's their fault." One direction is to blame everyone else, yet attributing all the blame to yourself, even when external factors play a significant role, is also wrong. Acknowledge and take responsibility for your actions and their impact on situations. Develop empathy, understand situations from others' perspectives, and be aware that outside factors you may not be privy to can influence the actions of others. I recommend using I statements. Instead of saying, "You made me feel." Instead, try "I feel" to express your emotions without placing blame. Also, instead of blaming, focus on finding a solution and moving forward. Actively challenge and reframe your thoughts that attribute blame to others without evidence.

SHOULD STATEMENTS

The 8th common cognitive distortion is should statements. "Should" is one of the most dangerous words you can use. A should statement sounds like an ironclad rule—only it's something you set for yourself and others without evaluating a circumstance.

The world has imposed shoulds all around us, setting us up to believe life and situations should be a certain way. Life should always be fair; it's unacceptable when bad things happen to good people. With a should statement, you tell yourself things should be a certain way with no exceptions. For example, you think your coworkers should always be on time, and those who are self-sufficient should always take care of themselves without asking for help. When it comes to yourself, you might believe you should always make your bed, or you should always make people laugh. When things don't work out as expected, you may constantly think, "I should be better." You may also be disappointed, feel guilty, frustrated, and let down. You may be using statements such as "I should go to the gym every day" as motivation, but every hour, circumstances change. And when you can't do what you should do, you become angry and upset. If, for example, you got out of work late and couldn't get to the gym, you could be upset and hold yourself to a "should" without acknowledging that you couldn't accommodate the gym because you didn't have time to go.

When reality does not align with strict expectations, the shoulds can apply to one's behavior, the behavior of others, or the state of the world in general. Creating unrealistic standards for yourself is a self-imposed "should" to avoid. In addition to not "shoulding" on yourself, it's wise not to impose shoulds on others and expect others to behave according to your values or standards. Statements like, "He should know how I feel without me having to say anything," or "If he cared about me, he would just understand," are inappropriate. Expecting a partner to always know what you need without communicating can lead to disappointment and conflict.

Have you evaluated your shoulds? Perhaps you believe you should be acknowledged and praised at work and feel undervalued when this doesn't happen. Then you sit and think about it, and you get depressed about it. This distortion can be devastating. Perhaps you hold yourself to unrealistically high standards, which can lead to feeling inadequate and low self-esteem. When you don't follow your should, the pressure of shoulds can contribute to anxiety, stress, and depression as they become rules upon the reality that you create. When you notice yourself using should statements, challenge them. Ask yourself if they are realistic and fair and what evidence supports or contradicts them. Replacing "should" with "prefer" or "would like" is less rigid and allows for more flexibility.

The ultimate hack against should statements is to be compassionate toward yourself and others. Understand that everyone has limitations, and falling short of ideal standards is okay. Make your expectations more realistic and attainable. Adjust your expectations. Instead of focusing on what should have happened or what should have been done, focus on what did happen and what can be learned from it. Do your best to focus on the positive. Practice being in the moment and accepting things as they are. If the burden of shoulds significantly impacts your well-being when you're constantly saying, "These people should be doing this," "This should be happening," "This person should have done that," I want you to evaluate that, and consider getting help or talking to someone. A therapist, coach, or good friend can help you become aware of the ways you're "shoulding" on yourself and help you challenge your should statements.

EMOTIONAL REASONING

The 9th common distortion is emotional reasoning. We're all guilty of it because it easily happens. Emotional reasoning is a cognitive distortion where individuals interpret their emotions as facts. Assuming that if they feel a certain way, the way they feel must be true. This way of thinking can lead to misinterpretations of situations and reinforce negative beliefs about yourself, others, and the world. When you're using emotional reasoning, it's easier to believe your feelings are a reflection of reality. For example, if you feel inadequate in a situation, with emotional reasoning, that discomfort soon becomes "I don't belong anywhere." With that thought, this cognitive distortion can cause you to think future events are impacted based on the way you feel now. For example, if you wake up feeling anxious, you may think something bad will happen today. Emotional reasoning can also cause you to make negative assumptions, concluding that you're being treated poorly if things don't go your way.

Have you fallen into this distortion? Believing that because you feel a certain way, it must reflect on the objective reality of a situation can be wrong. Yes, I teach you to follow your intuition and listen to your feelings. But if you follow your feelings 100%, you're missing other important information in making your decisions. Emotional reasoning can create a cycle where negative emotions lead to negative thoughts, intensifying the negative emotions. For example, feeling anxious about a social event and thinking, "I'm going to embarrass myself," increases your anxiety. This distortion often reinforces a negative self-image and contributes to low self-esteem. With emotional reasoning, you can feel like a failure and think, "I'm useless and can't do anything right." For instance, feeling unloved in a moment of conflict and concluding that your partner does not care about you at all can strain your relationship because of how you feel.

So, challenge your thoughts when you notice yourself engaging in emotional reasoning. Ask yourself if there is evidence to support or contradict your thought. Learn to observe your emotions as a neutral observer without immediately reacting. Understand that emotions are temporary and do not define you or your reality. What often happens is you have emotions that are a part of the shadow—part of deep, hidden subconscious beliefs that are not accurate to what is going on.

The easiest way to determine if something is coming from parts of deep subconscious programming is when you're feeling anxious about something for no reason. Because of these deep subconscious beliefs, you could also be scared and fearful about something for no reason. And then you think, "Well, I'm very anxious about this, so something is wrong." Instead of jumping to conclusions, learn to observe your emotions without immediately reacting to them. Try to use balanced thinking and look at situations from multiple perspectives rather than relying solely on your emotional response, which is still important. Learn to identify and express your emotions accurately and develop an emotional literacy. Positive affirmations can counteract negative thoughts that arise from emotional reasoning. That is one way to deprogram false beliefs within you that create these emotions directly.

FALLACY OF CHANGE

The 10th common cognitive distortion is the fallacy of change. The fallacy of change comes with an expectation that others must change to fit your expectations and needs. For example, you want your partner to focus only on you, despite knowing they've always been very social and value time with their friends. So, you tell them it's not okay with you whenever they go out. You imagine that, eventually, they will change their ways and want to stay home with you all the time. There's this belief that you can change someone and that they will change based on what you say. Believing that one's happiness or life circumstances depend on the actions and beliefs of others is wrong. By saying, "Oh, if only my spouse were more attentive, then I would be happy," you're placing unrealistic expectations on others, which changes their fundamental characteristics or behavior.

For instance, have you ever said, "My friend should know I need support right now and should be reaching out to me?" At the same time, you're mad they didn't reach out when they may not have any idea what's going on with you. This is an attempt to coerce or manipulate others into changing their behavior to align with your own needs or desires. You may believe, "If I act unhappy, maybe my partner will realize they need to spend more time with me," so you act unhappy all the time, and suddenly, your partner gets sick of it and they leave you.

Focus on how you can control your thoughts, feelings, and behaviors. There's no need for you to control others. Understand and accept that people have their values, personalities, and behaviors, which may not always align with your preferences. Set realistic expectations, and learn to accept others as they are rather than how you wish them to be. Instead of expecting others to know your needs and meet them, it's best if you communicate them clearly and directly. Concentrate on changes you can make in your behavior and reactions to navigate relationships and situations better. Focus on self-change, trying to understand others' perspectives and why they behave the way they do instead of attempting to control them. If the fallacy of change is significantly impacting your relationships and well-being, consider seeking support.

GLOBAL LABELING

The 11th common cognitive distortion is global labeling, which occurs when you take a single attribute and turn it into an absolute. Labeling involves an isolated event that is judged and then defined—usually as negative and extreme. For example, if you see a coworker checking her make-up before a meeting, you assume she's vain, can't meet deadlines, and is generally useless in the office. An extreme form of overgeneralization, global labeling judges an individual action without paying attention to the context, leading to assumptions, labels, and judgments that are likely inaccurate.

These inaccurate labels can hurt you and others. They negatively impact your self-esteem, causing depression, insecurity, and anxiety, and add friction to even the most stable relationships. Overgeneralization is wrong; you draw broad, generalized conclusions based on a single incident or a few incidents. When you label someone, usually it's negative and focused on perceived faults or shortcomings. Say you see someone act selfishly in a specific situation, and you label them as selfish in general. Applying global labels to yourself, often critically and harshly, can be very dangerous, and you say, "I am stupid." This is where you get the I am messages that are so powerful.

When you use global labeling, it leads to stereotyping and unfair judgments. When we witness a driver make a mistake, we don't say, "All young drivers are reckless," but this sort of distortion is happening all the time. When people say words and phrases like "all," "every one of those," and "they're all alike," then you know that you've gotten to this point of global labeling. When you notice yourself applying a global label, challenge it no matter what and ask yourself if the label you're assigning is based on sufficient evidence. If there are counter-examples, use specific language instead of global labels to describe specific behaviors. For example, instead of saying, "I'm a failure," you can say, "I made a mistake on this occasion." Be kind to yourself and others, and understand that everyone makes mistakes—one incident does not define anyone.

Encourage yourself to see the complexity in situations and people rather than reducing them to a single label. Make an effort to notice and appreciate positive qualities in yourself and others, and you'll start to lean less heavily on this common distortion of global labeling.

ALWAYS BEING RIGHT

The 12th common cognitive distortion is always being right, and I've been guilty of this. I have been guilty of every one of these distortions. The journey I went on to uncover these distortions has helped me immensely in truthfully seeing the world. I don't care how smart you are or how many books you read. You are not always right. If you want to flourish in life, you must be willing to say, "I am wrong," and admit that you do not know everything. If you have a persistent need to prove your beliefs and opinions are correct while dismissing and not considering the perspectives of others, this can lead to tragic consequences. When you hold on to your own beliefs, even in the face of contradictory evidence or the viewpoint of others, this flexibility is destroying you and the world.

Often, people believe they're always right, and then they only seek out the evidence they can find to prove that they're right. Then, once they've advertised their beliefs and opinions, they can never change their mind because they may be embarrassed. Insisting that your approach to a project, an idea, or whatever is the only correct one, despite what other alternative solutions have been presented, will always work against you, which is wrong. When you react defensively, when your opinions or actions are challenged, and you perceive it as a personal attack, this is distortion. It's just not true. If you believe you're always right, you lack empathy, and it will cause you to struggle to see or understand things from another person's perspective. Do not dismiss your partner's feelings during an argument, even if you believe them to be wrong, because it will lead to further arguments.

Do you need validation or constant affirmation from others that your views are correct? Why do you have this view? What is the reason for it? I've seen this in relationships and work environments. For self-perception and sound mental health, you must practice humility. Acknowledge that you do not have all the answers, and know it's okay to be wrong. Make a conscious effort to understand and validate others' perspectives, even when you disagree. Embrace your mistakes, and view mistakes as a chance to learn and grow instead of threatening your self-worth. Recognize that not every situation requires you to prove you are right. Sometimes, it is more beneficial to let go and move than continue arguing. You will never win the argument; you will always lose.

I recommend that you practice active listening and focus on truly listening to others without formulating a response while they're speaking. When people are talking, you're thinking of how you will respond and not actively listening to what they're saying. Oftentimes, you miss what they're saying because you're preoccupied with what you're going to say. If you actively seek out feedback on your behavior, it may help—just be open to feedback that says you're wrong. Maybe accepting this information will propel you to greater heights in consciousness and your life in general. I recommend you regularly reflect on your interactions with others and consider how insisting on being right may be affecting your relationships and well-being.

DISMANTLING YOUR DISTORTIONS

Cognitive distortions are prevalent everywhere, and it's something you have to come to grips with. I've given specific solutions for each of these 12 cognitive distortions, and we've repeatedly mentioned how being mindful and aware is one of the critical things you can do. You can also journal and write down your thoughts, especially negative ones, and identify if a particular cognitive distortion is at play. Over time, when you review your thoughts that you journal, you'll start to recognize patterns and distortions in your thinking.

Ask yourself the following questions:

- What is the evidence for and against this thought?

- Is there any other way to look at this situation?

Once you've identified the thoughts, distortions, and alternatives, you can replace distorted thoughts with more balanced and rational thoughts. Check to see if your thoughts and beliefs are accurate by checking them against facts and reality. Consider how others might view the situation to gain a more balanced perspective. Engage in actions that test the validity of your distorted thoughts. For example, if you believe you will fail a task, try it out and see what happens. Use the results of your experiments to adjust your thoughts and beliefs. Use positive affirmations and ensure your self-talk includes positive affirmations reinforcing your strengths and beliefs. Practices such as problem-solving, stress management, and resilience training can help your ability to masterfully respond to stress and adverse events.

AFFIRMATIONS—GET FREE FROM DISTORTIONS

Foster a growth mindset and embrace challenges. Seek support and practice gratitude and positivity. Educate yourself. Be open to new information that may contradict what you believe. Here are some affirmations you can use perhaps to change your way of thinking, and if you can adopt these ideas, they may help.

- I choose to see the whole picture, acknowledging both the positive and the negative.

- Life is full of gray areas, and I embrace the complexity of different situations.

- I accept that things can be both good and bad, and I learn from every experience.

- I give myself credit for my achievements and recognize my

strengths, positive experiences, and qualities as valid and significant in my life.

- I remain calm and grounded even in difficult situations.

- I focus on solutions rather than fearing the worst.

- I understand that not everything is about me, and I don't take things personally.

- I let go of the need for fairness, and I choose to create my own path.

- I understand that blaming others doesn't lead to growth or solutions.

- I replace "should" with "could" and empower myself to make choices.

- I accept others as they are. I'm only focused on changing myself.

- I see people in situations in their entirety, not just based on one aspect.

- I avoid labeling myself or others based on single events.

- I am open to being wrong and see the value in different perspectives.

- Being right is not as important as being understanding and compassionate.

There are dozens of cognitive distortions. We've only explored 12 of them. Addressing distortions is just as important as anything else in creating your reality. If you can understand, overcome, and dismantle these distortions, you will have the power to create the reality you choose without false distortions, taking you off the path toward your desired future. Creating the future you desire begins with granting yourself permission.

CHAPTER SEVEN

GRANT YOURSELF PERMISSION

"This Yes is about giving yourself the permission to shift the focus of what is a priority from what's good for you over to what makes you feel good."

—*Shonda Rhimes*

Imagine for a moment that you hold in your hand a key that has the power to unlock the doors to your dreams, aspirations, and true potential. What if I told you that this key is not held by someone else, nor is it out of reach? The key is right here in your grasp, waiting for you to use it.

This key is the permission to be who you truly are. To pursue your dreams with unwavering determination and to unleash your boundless potential.

You must grant yourself permission.

In this chapter, I'll delve into the profound significance of granting yourself permission—the barriers it helps you overcome and the limitless possibilities it opens. It is a journey of self-discovery and self-empowerment that begins with you saying right now, "I permit myself."

Through this discussion, we will unravel the mystery surrounding self-permission and understand why permission is not just an option but a necessity in our lives. We will explore the tangled web of self-limiting beliefs, the liberation that self-compassion brings, and the extraordinary heights that await those who dare to dream and permit themselves.

OBSTACLES TO PERMISSION

Let's take a moment to consider the reasons why we often hesitate to give ourselves permission. What holds us back from embracing our true selves and pursuing our passions with unyielding conviction? To understand the power of permitting ourselves, we must first recognize the self-limiting beliefs that shackled our potential.

These beliefs, often deeply ingrained, whisper in our ears, "You can't," "You shouldn't," or "You're not worthy." They create an invisible fence around our ambitions, dictating what we can and cannot achieve. As we embark on this journey, we will unveil these limiting beliefs, confront them head-on, and learn how to break free.

To learn the art of permitting yourself, you first must understand self-limiting beliefs. Self-limiting beliefs are like invisible chains that restrict your potential and hinder your personal development. There are those persistent, nagging thoughts that tell you you're not good enough, smart enough, or worthy enough to achieve your dreams.

These beliefs often stem from past experiences, societal expectations, or comparisons with others. The impact of self-limiting beliefs is profound. They can hold us back, keep us in our comfort zones, and prevent us from taking risks or pursuing our passions. They can make us settle for mediocrity when we're meant for greatness.

Let's take a moment to recognize some common examples of self-limiting beliefs I frequently hear:

- "I'm just not talented enough to succeed in that field."

- "I'm too old to start something new."

- "I'm ugly."

- "No one will love me."

- "I'm too old to be in a relationship."

- "What if I fail?"

- "Everyone will laugh at me."

- "I don't have the resources or connections to make it happen."

- "I should stick to what is safe and predictable."

Do any of these things sound familiar to you? I'm sure many of us can relate to one or more of these limiting thoughts. But remember, they're just thoughts. They're not truths.

These beliefs, if left unchallenged, can significantly hinder your progress. They create a self-imposed barrier, preventing you from seizing opportunities and pursuing your passions. We often find ourselves standing at the edge of greatness. We look out at the vast landscape of possibilities, but fear and self-doubt keep us from taking that crucial step forward. Imagine what could happen if you allowed these self-limiting beliefs to persist unchecked. Dreams would remain unfilled, talents hidden, and potential untapped. Regret becomes a constant companion, and the feeling of unfulfillment gnaws at your soul.

This is why understanding self-limiting beliefs is the first step to permitting yourself to unleash your true potential. But here's the good news. These beliefs are not fixed, unchangeable truths. They're merely stories we tell ourselves—and we have the power to rewrite those stories.

As we continue our exploration of self-permission, reflect on the self-limiting beliefs that may have held you back in the past or that you may be grappling with right now. Acknowledging these beliefs will take a significant stride toward embracing our full potential and living a life without unnecessary limits.

INCREASING SELF-WORTH

It's essential to understand why permitting yourself is so crucial in the first place. What about this act makes it a vital stepping stone on your path to personal growth and fulfillment?

To comprehend this, you must first acknowledge the external forces often discouraging self-permission. Your society, culture, and upbringing sometimes send subtle yet powerful messages suggesting you should play it safe, conform to the norm, and avoid rocking the boat.

From a young age, we are taught to follow the rules, meet certain expectations, and seek validation from external sources. We are conditioned to believe others must grant us permission or approval for our actions, decisions, and dreams. This external validation becomes a measure of our worthiness.

But what happens when you perpetually seek permission from external sources? Your dreams get put on hold, your desires are suppressed, and your authentic self is stifled. You become a spectator in your own life. Watching opportunities pass you by as you wait for someone else's approval while looking jealously at those who have given themselves permission and are living their lives as their authentic selves.

This is where the pivotal connection between self-permission and self-worth comes into play. When you depend on external validation, you unwittingly tie your self-worth to the opinions and judgments of others, and your self-esteem becomes fragile and vulnerable to the slightest critique or disapproval.

The act of granting yourself permission is a declaration of self-worth. It's an acknowledgment that your dreams, desires, and aspirations are valid simply because they are yours. It's a powerful affirmation that you are deserving of happiness, success, and fulfillment.

Let's take a moment to reflect on your life. Have there been instances where you sought permission from external sources, whether from family, friends, or societal norms? Have you ever hesitated to pursue a dream or passion because you were waiting for someone else's approval?

Oftentimes, we have done this in the past, and we are not even aware of it. Sometimes, we're not aware of our inner motivations. Recognizing the need for permission is not about dismissing external validation entirely. It's about realizing that the most important permission comes from within yourself. It's about understanding that you are the author of our destiny.

You must discover how to break free from the need for external validation and grant yourself the permission you deserve so you can stand tall in your authenticity and embrace your desires without hesitation.

BREAK THE BARRIERS

As you continue your exploration of self-permission, you arrive at a critical juncture, the moment when you confront and dismantle the barriers that hold you back from granting yourself the permission you so rightfully deserve.

So, how do you go about breaking down these barriers?

We've talked about self-limiting beliefs already, but we must identify them to fully break free from their grip. Think about an aspiration or a goal you've held back on. Now ask yourself:

- What's holding me back?

- What beliefs are preventing me from pursuing this dream?

Often, just acknowledging these beliefs is the first step towards dismantling them. Once identified, it's time to challenge them and question their validity. Ask yourself if these beliefs are based on facts or mere assumptions. More often than not, you'll realize they are built on shaky ground. With this understanding, their power over you diminishes.

Moving past self-limiting beliefs is a process of continually outwitting them and continuing to pursue your dreams despite failures and rejections that occur along the way. Some of the greatest writers encountered repeated rejections before making their big breaks.

Think of Frank Herbert, who was rejected 23 times before publishing the widely popular book "Dune." James Patterson was rejected 31 times before publishing the "Thomas Berryman Number," the first book in a series that made him one of the most popular writers in the world. Alex Haley received 200 rejections before seeing "Roots" in print. Jack London received 600 rejections before publishing his first story. If you've been rejected, you're in good company.

Consider the story of Malala Yousafzai, who defied societal norms and advocated for girls' education. Even in the face of grave danger, she permitted herself to speak out for what she believed in, and the world listened. Closer to home, think about the colleague or friend who decided to change careers, go back to school, or start their own business. Permission is the secret sauce that gave them the courage to pursue their passions.

These stories and millions of others illustrate that we all can break free from self-limiting beliefs and permit ourselves to pursue our dreams. These individuals are not exceptions. There are shining examples of what can happen when you choose to believe in yourself.

Remember that breaking down these barriers is a process that may not happen overnight. But every step forward, no matter how small, is a step towards liberation and freedom. As you continue this journey, you will discover that permitting yourself becomes not just a choice but a habit and a way of life.

The power to break down these barriers was hidden within you. Success is your birthright. And it's time to claim it. Permit yourself to be brave, bold, and believe in your capabilities.

TRANSFORM WITH SELF-COMPASSION

Another thing you must consider is the transformative power of self-compassion. Self-compassion, in its essence, is the practice of treating yourself with the same kindness, understanding, and empathy that you readily extend to others. It is the act of nurturing your well-being, especially during times of self-doubt or struggle—and self-compassion plays a profound role in your ability to permit yourself. Think of self-compassion as the gentle voice within that says, "It's okay to make mistakes, it's okay to have flaws, and you are worthy of love and kindness, just as you are." This self-compassionate perspective creates a safe space within to permit yourself to make mistakes, take risks, and pursue your dreams with courage.

What are the benefits of embracing self-compassion? First and foremost, it enables you to navigate the inevitable challenges and setbacks on your journey with resilience. Instead of harsher self-criticism, you can respond to difficulties with a nurturing attitude, which empowers us to bounce back stronger. Furthermore, self-compassion cultivates a positive and healthy self-image. Your self-image is what you see in the world around you, for everything around you is yourself pushed out. When you treat yourself with kindness, you build a foundation of self-worth that is not contingent on external validation. This sense of intrinsic worthiness bolsters your ability to permit yourself to pursue your passions and dreams.

Now, you might be wondering, "How can I cultivate self-compassion?" That's an excellent question, and the good news is that it's a skill that can be developed and strengthened.

One effective practice is to treat yourself as you would treat a close friend. When faced with a challenge or mistake, ask yourself, "What would I say to a friend in this situation?" Then, extend the same kind words of support to yourself. Another valuable exercise is self-compassionate self-talk. When you notice self-criticism creeping in, pause and reframe your inner dialogue and replace self-critical thoughts with self-compassionate ones. For example, instead of saying, "I'm such a failure," or "I'm so stupid," try saying, "I made a mistake, but that doesn't define my worth or potential."

When you practice self-compassion, you free yourself from the burden of self-criticism and create an environment where self-permission can flourish. Keep in mind that self-compassion is not a sign of weakness but a profound strength. It allows you to permit yourself to be human, to falter, and to grow.

You must remember this: be kind to yourself, permit yourself to be imperfect, and watch as your capacity for growth and self-empowerment expands beyond measure.

LIVING AN AUTHENTIC LIFE

As you journey deeper into the heart of self-permission, you arrive at the profound concept of self-acceptance, a fundamental pillar that supports your ability to permit yourself and live authentically.

Self-acceptance is the practice of fully embracing who you are, flaws and all. It's about recognizing that your mistakes, imperfections, or past does not define you. Rather, you are defined by your capacity to grow, evolve, love, and pursue your dreams with authenticity. Why is self-acceptance crucial on the path to self-permission? Because when you accept yourself unconditionally, you release the judgment and self-criticism that often holds you back. You permit yourself to be imperfect, to make mistakes, and to learn from them without the weight of shame or guilt.

So, how do you cultivate self-acceptance in your life? It begins with embracing both your strengths and weaknesses. Often, you are quick to acknowledge your strengths but hesitate to accept your weaknesses. However, it's important to remember that your shortcomings do not diminish your worth. They are growth opportunities to embrace our strengths. Take time to reflect on your accomplishments, talents, and the qualities that make you unique. Celebrate your achievements, no matter how small they may seem, and recognize that you have the capacity for greatness. Accept your weaknesses, and view them as areas for growth and development, not as limitations. Acknowledge that it's perfectly human to have limitations and understand that they do not define your potential. They offer opportunities for improvement and self-discovery.

You must understand unconditional self-love is the key. It's about treating yourself with the same love and compassion you would extend to a dear friend or loved one. When you love yourself unconditionally, you grant yourself permission to pursue your dreams—knowing you are deserving of success, happiness, and fulfillment. Self-love is not about arrogance, ego, or selfishness.

It's about recognizing your intrinsic worth and honoring it. It's about realizing that you are enough, just as you are. And you don't need external validation to prove your worthiness. It's important to understand that self-acceptance is not a destination but an ongoing journey. It's a journey of self-discovery and self-affirmation that evolves. There will be moments when self-doubt creeps in, but with self-acceptance as your compass, you can always find your way back to self-permission.

Remember that giving yourself permission is an act of self-love and self-respect. It's about saying to yourself, "I accept you. I love you, and I believe in you just as you are."

As you delve further and deeper into the heart of self-permission, you arrive at a place where, nurtured, and set free. This is the place where you discover the true freedom to dream. The act of giving yourself permission liberates your imagination and allows you to dream with audacity and purpose. It's about breaking free from the constraints of self-doubt and societal expectations and realizing that your dreams are not mere fantasies—they are the blueprints for your future realities.

When you give yourself permission, you open the door to daring to dream big. You give yourself the green light to envision a life beyond the ordinary to reach for the stars and create a reality that aligns with your deepest desires.

Throughout history, you find inspiring stories of individuals who dared to dream and transform the world. Consider the Wright brothers, who dared to believe that humans could fly and invented the first successful powered airplane. Or think of Martin Luther King Jr., who had a dream of a more just and equitable society and worked tirelessly to make it a reality. Closer to home, countless everyday heroes turned their dreams into reality.

Countless individuals started businesses, wrote books, pursued artistic passions, and made a difference in their communities because they dared to dream and permitted themselves to do so.

These stories should remind you that the freedom to dream is not a luxury. It's a fundamental human right. You can dream and have the power to turn those dreams into reality.

DREAMING BIG AND TAKING ACTION

Now, the challenge is to think about your most audacious dreams. What is it that sets your heart on fire? What vision do you hold in your mind's eye—even if it seems out of reach, even if you don't think you have permission to do it?

Giving yourself permission is not just about acknowledging your dreams. It's about pursuing them with unwavering determination. It's about taking that first step, no matter how small, toward the life you envision. It's about honoring the dreams and the compass that guide you toward a life of purpose, prosperity, and fulfillment.

When you permit yourself to dream, you become the architect of your destiny. You move from being passive observers of life to an active creator of your reality. You no longer allow circumstances or self-doubt to dictate your path. Instead, you chart your course with intention and passion.

Keep in mind that giving yourself permission is not an act of selfishness. It is not an act of service to self but self-love. It's about embracing your dreams and believing you are worthy of pursuing them. It's about permitting yourself to live a life that is truly yours, a life of purpose, passion, boundless potential, and service. Now, it's time to take those dreams off the shelf and breathe life into them through the unwavering force of action.

Dreams, no matter how grand or inspiring, remain unfulfilled until we take the critical step of action. Action is the ultimate form of prayer. Giving yourself permission is not merely about envisioning a better future; it's about actively participating in the creation of that future. Taking action is the bridge between where you are today and where you want to be tomorrow. It is the currency of progress, the vehicle of transformation, and the manifestation of your dreams in the physical world.

Taking action can be daunting. The fear of failure often looms, and procrastination can become a formidable obstacle. You may worry about making mistakes or facing setbacks, and this fear can paralyze you. But every great dream, every magnificent achievement, and every extraordinary success is built on a foundation of failures, setbacks, and mistakes. It is through these experiences that you learn, grow, and ultimately prevail.

So, how do you overcome the fear of failure and procrastination? One effective strategy is to break your goals into smaller, manageable steps. Taking one small step at a time makes the journey less overwhelming, and progress becomes tangible. Another powerful approach is to hold yourself accountable. Share your goals with a friend, mentor, or coach who can provide support and encouragement. Having someone to share your dreams with can make a significant difference in staying committed to your goals. Additionally, create a clear plan of action and define the specific steps you need to take to move closer to your dreams, then set deadlines and milestones to track your progress.

Remember, action is not about perfection. It's about progress.

Think about Thomas Edison, who failed countless times while trying to create the light bulb. We've heard this example many times, but Edison is a perfect example of permission—his relentless action and experimentation eventually led to success.

Reflect on the countless entrepreneurs who started with a dream and took consistent action to build successful businesses. These stories remind us that action is the catalyst for transformation. It's the engine that drives us toward our dreams. It's about having the courage to step into the unknown, face challenges head-on, and persist in pursuing what you truly desire.

Giving yourself permission is the beginning of the journey, but action is the path that leads you to your destination. Take that first step today. It doesn't matter how small or imperfect that step may be. What matters is that you permit yourself to start moving toward your dreams. Remember that the world is full of opportunities, and with each action you take, you bring your dreams closer to reality.

AFFIRMATIONS—GRANT YOURSELF PERMISSION

Many of you may think, "I'm permitting myself; I'm not limiting myself," but I promise there are many things in your life that you are not permitting yourself to do. I recommend repeating the following affirmations to yourself to open up this inner principle of giving yourself permission.

- I give myself permission to dream big and pursue my passions.

- I permit myself to trust in my abilities and believe in my potential to make my dreams a reality.

- I permit myself to have success, happiness, and fulfillment in every area of my life.

- I permit myself to feel worthy of achieving my dreams, and I am open to all the opportunities that come my way.

- I permit myself to let go of fear and welcome courage as my constant companion on this journey.

- I permit myself to be the author of my destiny, and I create a life that aligns with my deepest desires.

- I permit myself to commit to taking consistent and inspired action towards my dreams.

- I give myself permission to trust the timing of my life and remain patient as I work towards my goals.

- I permit myself to become a magnet for positive energy, and I attract the resources and support needed to achieve my dreams.

- I give myself permission to be resilient and overcome obstacles with grace and determination.

- I permit myself to celebrate my achievements, both big and small, as I progress towards my dreams.

- I permit myself to be grateful for the journey and appreciate every step that leads me closer to my dreams.

- I permit myself to live a life of authenticity, purpose, and fulfillment.

- I permit myself to be the source of my happiness and

success.

- I permit myself to feel the love, joy, and abundance that my dreams will bring.

Permission is the key that unlocks the door to the reality of your dreams, where the magic awaits.

CHAPTER EIGHT

BRING ME THE MAGIC

"And above all, watch with glittering eyes the whole world around you because the greatest secrets are always hidden in the most unlikely places. Those who don't believe in magic will never find it."

—*Roald Dahl*

Magic exists. It is all around you and most definitely within you. You find it in a realm—unseen and unfelt by many—but known intimately by those who dare to seek. In this chapter we'll discover the magic that's available and discuss ways to access it daily.

Every time this magical realm is activated, magical things happen in every moment. In this chapter, we'll explore what it takes to activate and live in this very magical realm. Have you ever felt a moment so pure, so inexplicably beautiful, that it took your breath away? Maybe it was a serendipitous meeting with an old friend, or perhaps it was the unexpected beauty of a sunset after a gloomy day.

Those moments are glimmers of magic.

Many of us go through our days, our lives, bogged down by routines, expectations, and the sheer weight of responsibilities. We forget to notice the magic. But what if it's not the world that lacks magic but your perception? You activate this magic when you hold the right frequency within and truly remember to tune into it. This magic isn't about literal spells and wands; it's about an inner vibration, a frequency of awe, wonder, and gratitude.

Every morning, when I wake up, I say, "Bring me the magic," and I want you to say that too. With those words, I set an intention to shift my frequency of interaction with the world in a way that looks for the magic in every moment. We live in a universe that resonates with energy and frequencies. Everything from the smallest atom to the largest galaxy vibrates.

Our thoughts, emotions, and intentions are no different when we truly look for magic. But, the more you seek magic, the more you find it. When you ask for magic and notice it, you are tuning yourself to a frequency where miraculous things manifest effortlessly. Imagine a day when you're so tuned into this magical frequency that miracles, as they are perceived, become an everyday affair. Gifts from the universe arrive as if out of thin air. You speak a desire, and before you know it, your desire appears. Moments after thinking, "I'd really love a mango right now," you pass by a fresh fruit stand on the side of the road selling freshly sliced mangoes. Suddenly, a solution to a problem you've been pondering is right in front of you.

These synchronicities aren't mere coincidence. It is an alignment with magic. Everything is already magic. The laughter of a child, the signposts that guide our paths, and the profound connections we share. Even in our very existence, you meet every single one of us. We are all part of this grand, wondrous tapestry of magic.

THE MAGIC OF MINDFULNESS

But how do you ensure that you stay attuned to this magical frequency? It begins with intention and awareness. The first thing is mindfulness. One of the most powerful tools at your disposal is mindfulness. It's not about emptying your mind but filling them with the present moment. By being truly present, we begin to notice the intricacies of the world around us, the way sunlight filters through the leaves, creating patterns of light and shadow, and the kind smile of a stranger passing by. With this attention, the world becomes richer and more vivid.

At its core, mindfulness is being fully present and engaged in the current moment without judgment. When combined with the idea of creating magic in our lives, mindfulness can become a transformative tool.

How do you create this mindfulness? Begin by truly immersing yourself in every task—whether sipping tea, walking, or conversing with a friend. By being wholly present, you unveil layers of experience previously unnoticed, like the intricate dance of steam from your tea or the blissful nature around you during a walk. This depth adds a touch of magic to the mundane. You can write a daily practice to list mentally or in a journal things you are grateful for. By focusing on abundance and blessings, you shift from a mindset of lack to one of appreciation.

Regularly reflect on the transient nature of experiences, emotions, and even challenges. By accepting impermanence, you'll find beauty and magic in the fleeting moments—a child's laughter, the brief bloom of a flower, and the transient hues of a sunset. Whenever you eat, walk, or even rest, consciously engage all your senses. What do you see, hear, feel, taste, and smell? By fully experiencing the world through your senses, you deepen your connection to your surroundings. Making everyday experiences feel enchanted.

Set clear intentions for what you desire. Visualize the outcome, feel the emotions associated with that wonderful experience, and then release it to the universe with trust. This process harnesses the power of focused intention, and it turns abstract desires into tangible realities. Akin to weaving magic, spend time outdoors, but do so mindfully feel the earth under your feet. Listen to the birds and observe the rhythm of nature. Nature is inherently magical when you immerse yourself in its rhythm. You sync with its energy, invoking a sense of wonder and serenity. Rather than being swayed by every thought or emotion, practice observing each emotion non-judgmentally, seeing them as passing clouds and detaching from turbulent thoughts and feelings.

Through this practice, you allow space to access a serene inner space, a sanctuary where true magic resides. When conversing with someone who truly listens without crafting your response, hear not just the words but emotions and unspoken sentiments. And this deep connection will foster understanding and empathy, making ordinary conversations magical and exchanging energy and insight.

Throughout the day, take moments to focus solely on your breathing. Feel the rise and fall of your chest. The air is a journey and its rhythm. Breath is life; by focusing on it, you connect with the elemental magic of existence.

Recognize and celebrate small achievements and joys. No matter how trivial they might seem. Celebration cultivates a mindset of abundance and joy, turning everyday accomplishments into magical milestones. Remember, the essence of magic in this context is the profound beauty, wonder, and interconnectedness in life that goes unnoticed. By practicing mindfulness, you sharpen your perception and align these magical elements—transforming your inner and external experiences.

THE GLORY IN GRATITUDE

Another key to bringing the magic to you is gratitude. Magic often manifests in the small, everyday moments. By expressing gratitude for even the smallest moments, we amplify their magic. A simple "Thank you" to the universe can work wonders. The acknowledgment reminds us of the blessings we have and opens our hearts to receive even more magic.

Gratitude is an incredibly potent tool. When we talk about creating magic through gratitude, we're referring to the transformative and enriching shifts in our lives that arise from a sustained practice of appreciation. By focusing on what you're thankful for, you begin to shift your perspective from what's lacking or challenging to what's abundant and positive in your life. This change in perception attracts more positive experiences. It says that life begins to mirror back the abundance that you acknowledge.

Gratitude is a high-frequency emotion. And when you genuinely feel grateful, you radiate vibrant energy. Because like attracts like, when you're resonating at this elevated frequency, you magnetically attract experiences, people, and opportunities that align with this vibration. Embracing gratitude during challenging times is a balm for emotional wounds and anxieties. Healing and self-growth are magical processes. And by using gratitude as a tool, you accelerate this journey—often uncovering hidden strengths and insights along the way.

Expressing gratitude towards people strengthens bonds and nurtures trust. Enhanced relationships are magical. In themselves, they open doors to deeper understanding, shared joys, and the collective creation of cherished memories. A grateful mindset makes you more receptive to recognizing and receiving unexpected blessings, inviting serendipities, and strengthening connections. From this place, life begins to surprise you with serendipities and coincidences that feel like the universe's way of winking at you in this magical realm. Gratitude grounds you in the present moment and makes you deeply aware of your current blessings.

Self-awareness is a magical key that unlocks your personal growth, deeper relationships, and authentic living. Gratitude amplifies your joy and wonder for life's simpler pleasures. This consistent joy infuses everyday experiences with a sense of magic, making the ordinary feel extraordinary. In essence, gratitude acts as a bridge, connecting you to the magic that's always been present but often overlooked. By intentionally cultivating and expressing gratitude, you fine-tune your senses, perceptions, and energies, making you both the conduits and creators of magic in your life.

SEEK MAGIC

Ask for magic and actively seek out the magic in your day. Challenge yourself to find three magical moments every day. It can be as simple as a bird song or a kind gesture from a colleague. Over time, you'll find that these moments multiply. It's amazing what you will find. Actively seeking the magic is part of the key to experiencing this magical realm. Active seeking implies a proactive approach and intentional effort to search, recognize, and harness the elements of magic in our lives. The idea is not just to be passive recipients but to actively cultivate and nurture magical moments and experiences.

You can use active seeking to bring magic into your life. Firstly, begin each day by setting a clear intention to find and experience the magic. The intention might be as simple as saying, "Today, I will find magic in nature and with a clear intention." Through this affirmation, your focus sharpens, making you more attuned to magical experiences aligned with that intention.

Journaling is another way to seek magic. I recommend keeping a magic journal every day to jot down moments, experiences, or realizations that felt magical. Over time, this practice heightens your awareness of magic and creates a rich tapestry of magical memories. Create daily or weekly rituals such as meditating at sunrise, walking in nature, or lighting a candle while expressing gratitude. These rituals, for some reason, imbibe everyday actions with intention and reverence, transforming them into magical experiences.

There is magic in learning. Actively seeking new knowledge or skills has magic in it, be it a dance class, a pottery workshop, an art class, or diving into mystical literature. Learning is an alchemical process, turning the unknown into the known, creating magic through discovery and mastery.

Engage in activities like art, music, or gardening with full presence. Lose yourself in the process. When you're wholly absorbed, time seems to stand still, everything becomes magical, and you've entered into that magical realm.

Pay attention to coincidences, patterns, and synchronicities in life. Recognize these winks from the universe. It adds a layer of wonder and mystery and reminds you of the magic in the ever-present moment.

Actively seek and engage with individuals or communities who share your belief in magic. Shared beliefs and experiences amplify the sense of magic—creating a collective energy that's both supportive and inspiring.

Actively seek opportunities to give, be a time resource, or just be a listening ear for others. Giving selflessly creates a ripple of magic, touching lives and returning to you tenfold.

THE SUBTLETY OF MAGIC

Sometimes, magic doesn't appear instantly. Sometimes, it's subtle. Sometimes, it waits around the corner. But the magic is always there, especially when you trust its presence and timing. Imagine if each of us tapped into this magic daily. The collective energy and shared frequency would be powerful enough to bring about incredible transformations, not just in our personal lives but in the world.

In ancient times, magic was seen as a direct link between humanity and the Divine—a way to communicate with the cosmos. Today, while our understanding of the universe has expanded, the core idea remains. Magic is our bridge to the sublime. The extreme ordinary amidst the ordinary. So, as you continue your journey, remember that every day holds the potential for magic. Embrace it, cherish it, and above all, be a beacon of it. And when life's challenges seem overwhelming, take a moment to breathe deeply and gently remind yourself, "Bring me the magic." Your days will be filled with wonder, your nights with dreams of possibility, and your life with the unmistakable touch of magic.

There is an old saying to the believer, "No explanation is necessary." To the non-believer, "No explanation is possible." This is often how magic operates in our lives. But if we reframe our understanding, instead of seeing magic as mere unexplained phenomena, we see it as the essence of life itself.

You must embrace the subtle magic. Life's magic doesn't always manifest in grand, earth-shattering moments. More often than not, it's found in the subtleties, the quiet moments that are easy to overlook. Look for nature's whispers, the gentle rustle of leaves, the mesmerizing dance of fireflies on a summer night, or the rhythmic sounds of waves crashing on a shoreline. Each of these natural wonders is a manifestation of the universe's magic we can tap into. One doesn't need to do anything grandiose. Simply being present, listening, and observing can connect us to the magic around us.

Magic is about human connections. Have you ever thought of someone, and they call or message you out of the blue? Or, perhaps, you've been in a situation where a stranger offered assistance just when you needed it.

These aren't mere coincidences but a testament to the interconnectedness of all of us. Our energies or frequencies often intertwine in ways we can't comprehend but can surely appreciate. You are becoming a catalyst for magic at this moment. As you become more attuned to the magic in your life, you can also become a channel and catalyst for it. It starts with intentional living and starting each day with a clear intention. It doesn't necessarily mean a to-do list but rather a feeling or a state of being you'd like to embody. Perhaps it's joy, kindness, or adventure. By setting this intention, you're priming yourself to experience and spread this particular form of magic.

The universe often works in a give-and-take rhythm, and when we offer acts of kindness, not only do we make someone's day brighter, but we also align ourselves with positive frequencies. And as many can attest, what we give often comes back to us tenfold.

Carl Jung, the famous psychologist, spoke of synchronicities—meaningful coincidences that seem to defy pure chance. These events are unrelated happenings that converge in a meaningful manner or another layer of life's magic. They remind us there's more to our existence than meets the eye. Being open to and acknowledging these synchronicities can lead to profound realizations and transformative experiences.

Magic isn't something confined to fairy tales or ancient legends. It's an integral part of your existence. It's in the air you breathe, the connections you forge, and the dreams you dare to dream. It is your role to recognize, honor, and dance to its timeless rhythm. Curiosity is where magic exists, and it's been waiting for you all along. Magic, in essence, is the tapestry of reality woven with threads of wonder, synchronicity, and unseen connections. Each of us is both a weaver and a thread within this vast experience.

QUANTUM EMOTIONS

If we were to look at the universe through the lens of quantum physics, we would see that the very fabric of reality is teeming with possibilities and potentialities. Particles exist in states of probability until they're observed. This phenomenon suggests that the very act of observing or paying attention brings forth a certain reality from a realm of potential.

Like a quantum observer, we collapse the wave of potential into the tangible experience of magic. Emotions play a pivotal role in our experience of magic. They are the colors with which we paint our perceptions. When we feel joy, gratitude, or love, we are in harmony with positive frequencies. This resonance is a magnet drawing in experiences and moments that align with these emotions.

Think of the last time you felt genuinely happy. Didn't everything seem to fall into place in the world to appear more vibrant and more alive? That's emotional magic at work. Stories have been our bridge to the magical as well. Through tales, myths, and legends, we've passed down experiences of the mystical, the unexplained, and the wondrous. The stories we tell ourselves and others shape our reality. If your inner narrative is one of wonder and curiosity, your external experiences will mirror that. By choosing to see yourself as a character in a grand magical tale, you open the doors to enchantment.

When we as a group focus on a shared goal, magic amplifies. It's why group meditations on Saturdays or collective prayers have profound impacts. It's the coming together of multiple frequencies harmonizing into a potent force of true magic.

COLLECTIVE MAGIC

The depth and breadth of magic in your life is boundless. It's a spectrum that spans from the subtle whispers of nature to the profound realizations of quantum mechanics. Every facet of our existence, every emotion, every story, and every connection hold the potential for magic. So, as you traverse life, remember that magic isn't just around you; it's within you. It's the heartbeat of the cosmos echoing in your soul, the dance of particles in every breath, and the weave of stories in every moment. Embrace it, nurture it, and let it illuminate your path.

Imagine life as a series of concentric circles, each representing a layer of your experience. At the core is our inner self, and as you move outward, the circles encompass your relationships, community, environment, and finally, the cosmos. Magic flows through each of these circles—manifesting uniquely in every layer.

I find magic in the inner sanctum of my dreams and intuition—the magic of self-awareness. The subconscious mind often communicates with you through dreams and intuitive nudges. If you had a dream that felt prophetic or a sudden gut feeling that guided you away from harm, this is the magic of your higher self speaking to you. Every time you overcome a challenge or learn a new skill, there's a touch of magic in it. The human capacity to grow and adapt is nothing short of miraculous.

There are times when you sense a loved one's emotions without a word being spoken, or you think of someone just as they call. This empathic bond is a testament to the invisible thread that connects us. Throughout our lives, we meet countless people, but there are some whose paths we crossed just at the right moment, leading to life-changing encounters. This serendipity is a dance of cosmic magic. Every culture has rituals, festivals, and traditions that celebrate life's magic. The lantern festivals of Asia and midsummer celebrations of Europe are collective expressions of magic in times of crisis. Often, we see communities come together in miraculous ways, like a neighborhood supporting a family in need or an entire nation rallying behind a cause. This unity amplifies the magic of collective consciousness.

The changing of seasons, each with its unique beauty and significance, is nature's rhythmic magic. The rebirth in spring, the abundance of summer, the transformation of fall, and the stillness of winter offer a lesson and a magic of their own. I love to find magic in the animals around me. The animals that come into my life are the birds, the rats, the chipmunks, and the raccoons.

Throughout history, various cultures have believed in animal spirits or guides. A chance encounter with a majestic eagle or curious fox can be seen as nature communicating its wisdom. Just look out into the cosmos, into the universe, and space, and you'll see magic right now. Events like solar eclipses and meteor showers or the dance of northern lights are always a reminder to me of the universe's grandeur and magic.

Have you ever felt a personal connection to a celestial event or found guidance in the patterns of stars? The cosmos often speaks to those who listen. Throughout the universe, magic weaves its way through every particle, every color, and every pattern. It's not just an external force; it's an intrinsic part of who you are and how you relate to the world. As you navigate the many circles of your life, let the magic be your compass—guiding you toward experiences and moments that resonate with your soul's purpose. Remember, every day, every moment is ripe with potential—the magic is there waiting for you to uncover, embrace, and let it transform your journey.

AFFIRMATIONS—BRING ME THE MAGIC

The dimension of magic is now the dimension of reality for you. And as you go out into the day, you'll see this magic around you. Here are some magical affirmations to help you assume that everything around you is magical and experience the magic of this moment.

- Bring me the magic.

- The magic within me is a powerful force that guides and uplifts my spirit.

- Each moment I breathe is a magical gift full of potential and surprise.

- I am in harmony with the magic of the universe, and its currents flow through me.

- With intention and belief, I manifest magic in every facet of my life.

- I am attuned to the magic of nature, feeling its pulse and rhythm in my soul.

- Magic is limitless, and so is my potential to create, dream, and achieve.

- With the alchemy of my emotions, I transform challenges into magical opportunities.

- My heart recognizes and responds to the magical connections that bind us all.

- Magic guides my path, leading me to serendipities and synchronicities.

- I trust in the universe's magical plan for me, knowing it's always for my highest good.

- I view the world with eyes of wonder, always ready to discover its hidden magic.

- Every exchange of energy with others is an opportunity to weave magic into our collective story.

- The magic of my dreams illuminates my waking life, guiding and inspiring me.

- Every moment in my life is touched by magic.

Inviting magic in your life and following the synchronicity it brings is a great way to cultivate your desired reality. It's essential that you stay committed to your path to continue to experience magic.

CHAPTER NINE

LET NOTHING DETER YOU

"Believe in your heart that you're meant to live a life full of passion, purpose, magic and miracles."

—Roy T. Bennett

You must not let anything deter you. A part of this process seems to be that there will be attempts to prevent you from manifesting what you truly want. This chapter will explore what it looks and feels like to live free of determent. When you set your sights on what Napoleon Hill calls your "definite chief aim," you must not let anything deter you. Now, that sounds cliche. Well, of course, you wouldn't choose to be deterred. But let me tell you the story of Eva and Elijah to give you an example to help you understand this message better.

Eva lived in a quiet town where the willows whispered in the days and meandered into each other like the gentle flow of a river. She lived as a woman with eyes the color of the stormy sea and dreams as vast as the night sky. Everyone knew her as the owner of The

Whisperings Pines, a quaint little bookstore between the bakery and the old mill. Yet within Eva, behind the facade of contentment, lay a treasure trove of canvases and colors. Eva was an artist. However, no one in this town had ever seen her art. Her dreams were painted in bold strokes and vibrant hues, drawn from the palette of her heart's deepest desires. She envisioned her art adorning the stark walls of galleries and the intimate corners of coffee shops, speaking silently to the souls who passed by. But over time, those dreams were meticulously folded away, like the delicate butterfly wings tucked within a cocoon, safe from the world's prying eyes and piercing judgments.

Unfortunately, Eva was deterred from following her dreams. Her spirit had been told not by a single cataclysmic event but by a relentless drizzle of doubt that seeped through the seams of her resolve. It began with her father's well-meaning but dismissive remarks, "Art is a difficult life, Eva. You should stick to the books." The discouragement was compounded by her love, who left her heart in tatters and scoffed at her aspirations, branding them as "childish fantasies."

Each morning before leaving for work, Eva would glance at the closed door of her studio, where her untouched canvases lay in wait, the aching chasm between her reality and her dreams— always widening every day she would go to work, and every day she simply would not paint what was in her heart. The stifled creativity was like a silent scream within her. Eva's days unfurled with the predictability of the seasons, each one a mirror of the last; the lure of her art, once a vibrant flame, slowly dimmed to a mere flicker choked by apprehension and the whispers of doubt that slithered through her thoughts and deterred her from following her goals.

Once upon a time, Eva was a vessel of dreams, brimming with the elixir of potential, but the voices around her dripping with the venom of criticism reached and blocked her will. "What a quaint hobby," or worse, well-meaning friends would remark. Eva is a darling artist for those who have the luxury of time as if her dreams were indulgent trifles, not necessities like air or water. Time became a weapon and a shield. There was never enough of it, she told herself. In truth, the expanse of hours and the

weight of starting daunted her. The blank canvas was an ocean and her confidence in the ship that had long ago sunk to its depths. Then there was the specter of failure, its ghastly fingers prying into her resolve. Failure haunted the quiet moments, whispering tales of public shame or efforts laid bare only to be dissected and discarded. "What if I'm simply not good enough?" she would wonder, "What if I'm just an impostor?"

The fear rooted itself deep and twined around her heart. It told her to be sensible and accept the comfort of the known. Art was the wild sea, and Eva convinced herself she was no longer made for such voyages. Ultimately, she built a fortress of routine around her, each brick a reason to stay hidden, to keep the colors of her soul neatly kept and the brushes dry. The world would turn, a silent guardian of dreams, deferred her canvas, blank and waiting for courage that has yet to come.

Then there's the story of Elijah who held unyielding determination. His journey was of tenacity. He did not let anything deter him on his journey. As a boy, Elijah gazed upon skyscrapers from the windows of his humble home, a cramped apartment he shared with his mother. With its ceaseless rhythm and promise of possibility, the city hummed a song, crafting visions of a life beyond the confines of need and the clutches of mediocrity. His dreams were audacious, his aspirations as vast as the ocean. He dreamt of education in business and leaving an indelible mark on the world. He dreamed of owning his skyscrapers and positively changing the world. He dreamed of starting foundations and helping the poor.

But Elijah soon learned his dreams were not enough. They needed to be clad in the armor of action, propelled by the engines of unwavering resolve. The doubts of others were the first dragons he slew voices that deemed his goals too lofty for a boy of his station. However, his heart beat to the rhythm of his convictions. Elijah consumed knowledge with a voracious appetite, each book a stepping stone across the river of "can'ts and shouldn'ts," financial hurdles towered like giants. While many would be deterred from these hurdles, while their shadows loomed over his college aspirations, Elijah toiled his nights under the glow of streetlamps, his hands calloused from work, his mind resolute, letting nothing deter him. Scholarships were his slingshot, and the giants fell one by one, paving the way to his academic conquest.

In business, failure loomed like a ghost always trying to deter him. It's whispers seeping into entrepreneurial ventures. He faced it with a grin, for he knew that failure was not the antithesis of success, but it was a crucible. Each failed attempt was a lesson etched into the blueprint of his ambition, each rejection a detour, not a dead end. He let nothing deter him. Obstacles became opportunities, and doubts became the fuel for his inner fire. When told his ideas were too unconventional, he remembered the skyscrapers, those marvels of human ingenuity, and pressed on.

He crafted a business that mirrored his heart and was innovative, resilient, and impactful. He started foundations, and he helped children. He realized all of his dreams as he had imagined them.

Time and again, he would encounter the naysayers and the cynics who saw the world through the lens of limitation and lack. He offered a smile, for he knew a secret. The pessimists were not the architects of his reality. At his command, Elijah's life unfolded like an epic saga, where the hero's triumph is not by the sword but by the unassailable strength of his imagination. His goals, once distant stars, became the sun that lit his day, each wish fulfilling a world he had brought into being. And so, he stood amidst the city's relentless pull, a living testament to the creed that had guided his every step: let nothing deter you.

TAPPING INTO DETERMINATION

You may not even be aware of the ways that you are being deterred. Within each person lies a capacity for overcoming any obstacle. This power resides not in the muscles or the physical world but in the vast untapped resources of your subconscious mind. I am imploring you to harness this inner strength to rise in the face of envy, diversity, and deterrence.

What are the types of deterrence I'm mentioning? They are the fears, the hesitations, and the naysayers that whisper of impossibility. They are the failures of yesterday that threaten to overshadow tomorrow's potential. They are the societal norms that confine you to the ordinary when you are indeed built for the extraordinary. Your first step in overcoming these barriers is to recognize them. We must shine a light on our doubts and fears. For in the light, they lose their power. Acknowledge them not as truths but as illusions and shadows cast by the brilliance of our potential. The mind is a fertile garden. Whatever you plant—be it the seeds of success or the weeds of defeat—it will grow. You must cultivate your garden with positive affirmations, nurturing thoughts of success, happiness, and peace.

Your mind's focus dictates your reality. If you fixate on the hurdles, they will multiply. But if you set your sights on the victories, no matter how small, your path will be paved with triumphs. Your imagination is the very gateway to the reality you wish to create. It is the crucible within which all your desires are forged into existence. Yet, in pursuing goals, many often find themselves besieged by an onslaught of mental adversaries. These adversaries take the form of doubts, the negative opinions of others, past failures, and societal constraints. They are the shadows cast by our fears, the echoes of a world that tells us more about our limitations than our potential. We must transcend these ephemeral shadows to realize they are mere illusions conjured by our misdirected thoughts.

The difference between those who succeed and those who do not is not the absence of obstacles but the presence of persistence. It is the mindset that sees opportunity in adversity, learning in failure, and growth in challenges. In pursuit of your goal, you will often encounter barriers, the fear of failure, the fear of judgment, and sometimes even the fear of success itself. These fears can paralyze you, just as they did for me. They can trick you into believing that you're not good enough, you're not smart enough, or that your dream is not meant to be. I implore you to ask yourself, "What would I do if I wasn't afraid?" It's not just about eliminating fears. It's about not letting those fears control you. Instead, it's about harnessing that fear and turning it into the fuel for your journey.

You have the power of decision. Every moment is an opportunity to make a new choice. You can choose to act despite fear, commit, and recommit to your path every day. The power of focus is your greatest ally. Focus on what you can control: your effort, attitude, and mindset. By shifting your focus from what you lack to what you have, from what you can't do to what you can do, you move from being a passive player to an active creator in your life story.

Action is important. You must not be deterred from taking action. Success is not a stroke of luck or a gift of fate. It's the product of relentless action, not random but strategic action. This means knowing your purpose, knowing your outcome, and then taking massive, determined steps toward it daily without being deterred. We often stand at the precipice of action, waiting on the edge of "What if?" and "If only?" We've been conditioned to see the chasm as a void and abyss that swallows dreams and regurgitates regret. But what if we choose to see it differently? What if the chasm is not a void but a canvas, not an abyss but an altar of transformation? We are told that to achieve our goals, we must be relentless and that success is a fortress we must besiege. What if success is not a fortress but a horizon? Always ahead, always within sight, always within reach if we keep moving forward.

It's about motion, action, the alchemy of will and imagination. It's about the courage to act despite the paralysis of perfection, having the audacity to fail forward, and treating every setback as a setup for a comeback. The mind can be our greatest ally or most formidable adversary. It can conjure demons of doubt or deities of determination. So we must choose our allegiance not with trepidation but with the audacity of those who dare to dream out loud. To let nothing deter you is to embrace the quantum leap of faith and recognize that your actions can turn chaos into order, noise into music, and dreams into reality.

Just think for a moment about your life up to this point. The efforts to achieve your goals were likely littered with external and internal roadblocks. You encounter the naysayer who casts the shadows of doubt, the societal norms, the prescriber-sedated conformity, and inner critics that echo your deepest insecurities. These are the sentinels of the status quo, the guardians at the gates of greatness. The only true barriers that exist are those we place upon ourselves; they are the limits we accept as real. It is a fundamental law of the mind that we expect defeat. We are inevitably drawn to it. The antidote, then, is to shift the paradigm to alter the frequency of our thoughts to match that of our aspirations. It's about embodying the vibrational essence of our goals, aligning ourselves so fully with our intentions that the universe can't help but yield to our design.

Persistence toward your goals is not merely about positive thinking—it's the alchemy of transforming thought into substance. The disciplined application of focus and emotion, coupled with the unwavering commitment to action, transmutes desire into reality. It's a matter of tuning into the reality where your goals are already accomplished. Letting that vision guide every step and decision and letting nothing deter you is to walk through the world as a force of nature, with a magnetic pull that bends reality towards your will. It's to recognize that within you lies an untapped reservoir of potential, a quantum field of all possibilities, where you are the master, the creator, the Divine sculptor of your experience.

RESOLVE TO SUCCEED

As you move through life, do so with the steadfast resolve that your vision will manifest undeterred. You must act with the certainty that for every dream that burns within you, there is a corresponding power to achieve it. And with each action taken, affirm that you are moving closer to realizing your dreams.

Embrace the journey with passion, love, and relentless drive that allows no opposition. Let your life be a testament to the power of unwavering intent. Let nothing deter you from self-empowerment and transformation. The only compass to follow is the one that points to your true north, your unlimited potential.

"Let nothing deter you." It is not just a statement. It is a lived experience. The human mind is a living landscape of infinite potential, a frontier where your beliefs shape the topography of your life. Yet, it is also where you encounter the most formidable barriers. These barriers come in the form of conditioned thoughts—the habitual patterns that tell you that your dreams are too big, your abilities too small, or your timing not quite right. These are the echoes of a past self, a self not yet awakened to its power. These patterns are only neurological loop circuits in your brain firing in the same sequence—again and again, creating a familiar but limiting reality. To let nothing deter you, you must break these loops. You must forge new pathways, new sequences that align with the vision of the life you aspire to live.

How do you achieve this? You begin by cultivating a clear intention, a vivid and real vision that leaves no room for doubt. This vision is fueled by elevated emotions of joy, gratitude, and love for the reality you are about to manifest. This powerful combination of intention and emotion is the key to unlocking a new state of being. It is not enough to know this intellectually. You must embody it and step into the new self, the self who has already overcome the barriers and has achieved the goal. You must create from a place of abundance, not lack—from a place of possibility, not limitation.

To let nothing deter you is to understand that every challenge is an opportunity to evolve, grow, and become more of who you truly are. It is to recognize that the power to change any aspect of your life is always within you in the present moment. It is to commit to this change, not just in thought but in action. Let us all embrace the power within us to create, change, and transcend.

The world is watching in wonder as you transform the leaden weight of doubt into the gold of action. This is your charge, your challenge, your chorus. Let nothing deter you. Every breath is a declaration of intent and, every day, a step towards realizing our wildest imaginings.

To let nothing deter you, you must embrace the power of adaptability. Success is not a straight line. It's a winding road with detours and roadblocks. You have to be flexible in your approach. If you're committing to your outcome, you must be willing to change your approach as many times as necessary until you achieve it.

With all its seeming obstacles, the external world is but a reflection of your inner state. Change the inner state, the feeling, and the world itself transforms before your eyes.

Use your gift of imagination, not as a mere daydream but as a tool. When married with the certainty of feeling, the power of your mind becomes an unstoppable force. If you can conceive and believe with unwavering faith, you can and will achieve it. Cast aside the deterring whispers of impossible, impractical, or unrealistic. Instead, affirm that what you desire is not only possible but already in the process of becoming.

Make the vision of your goal so vivid, so real in the sanctuary of your silence that nothing can shake it.

Your conviction must become a living, breathing entity immune to the vagaries of circumstance. Commit to this path of undeterred creation. Assume the feeling of your wish being fulfilled and act from that state. And as you do, remember reality is not a fixed fate but a limitless range of possibilities. Armed with your imagination, let nothing and no one deter you from realizing those endless possibilities. Practice the art of mental discipline. Train your subconscious mind to be a collaborator. Feed it with the wisdom of positivity, the knowledge of your worth, and the conviction that no external circumstance can dictate your potential. Visualize your goals with such clarity and frequency that your subconscious works tirelessly to manifest that reality. That is how you keep from being deterred.

Remember, success doesn't mean there are no failures. Success is the persistence **through** failure. Every setback is a setup for a comeback. The Phoenix rises from ashes, not the pristine ground with unscathed feathers. Let nothing deter you. Not the ridicule of skeptics nor the whisper of self-doubt. You are the master of your destiny. You can influence, direct, and control your environment. You can make your life what you want it to be. Your mind is the canvas, belief, the brush, and the paint.

In writing your life story, you must write with a pen dipped in the ink of courage, drawing lines that map the terrain of your highest aspirations. Do not be waylaid by the mirage of immediate gratification, nor be swayed by the specter of failure which haunts the periphery of all great endeavors where it is in the pursuit, the reaching beyond your grasp where the essence of living is distilled.

Let nothing deter you. When the world beckons you to tread the worn path, may you have the fortitude to forge your own. When fear whispers that your dreams are folly, may you have the wisdom to listen instead to the sound of knowing your soul. And when the chapter of your life is read, may it tell of a journey undeterred, a summit attained in a legacy of indomitable spirit etched into the annals of time.

AFFIRMATIONS—LET NOTHING DETER YOU

Here are some affirmations you can say to yourself if you find that you're deterred from acting upon or achieving your goal.

- I am resilient, steadfast, and immune to discouragement.

- Every obstacle I face is a stepping stone to greater success.

- My determination is stronger than any doubt.

- I am focused, driven, and unstoppable in my journey.

- Challenges have strengthened my resolve and sharpened my focus.

- I embrace difficulties as opportunities to demonstrate my tenacity.

- Nothing can deter my spirit.

- I am filled with the strength and vision of the infinite, and I let nothing deter me from my goals.

- My mind is aligned with Divine wisdom.

- The perfect plan is now revealed to me, and I follow it unwaveringly.

- I am surrounded by Divine protection, and no negative thoughts can take root in my mind.

- My subconscious mind is receptive to my desires, providing me with the knowledge and resources needed for success.

- The universe's wisdom makes me unstoppable in my journey toward my goals.

- I am steadfast in my actions and beliefs.

- The opinions of others do not sway my Divine purpose.

Let nothing deter you, and ensure the stories you tell yourself keep you committed to your progress.

CHAPTER TEN

WHAT STORY ARE YOU TELLING YOURSELF

"It's like everyone tells a story about themselves inside their own head. Always. All the time. That story makes you what you are. We build ourselves out of that story."

—*Patrick Rothfuss*

Think of your life as a grand narrative, a story where you are the hero at the center. Each day, with every thought, decision, and action, you are writing this epic tale. But have you ever stopped to ask yourself, "Am I writing a story that uplifts, empowers, and propels me toward my greatest potential?" This chapter is your guide to doing just that. It's about seizing the pen that writes the script of your life and becoming the master storyteller of your journey. You have the power to change the plot, transform the challenges into stepping stones, and turn the narrative of limitation into a narrative of limitless possibilities.

Your current story might be fraught with doubts, fears, and

limitations. It may be a tale of unfulfilled dreams or paths not taken. But what if I told you that you have the power to rewrite it? What if you could change your story from struggle to strength, from fear to courage, from complacency to relentless pursuit of your passion?

The process starts with belief. Believe in the possibility of change. Believe in the power of your intentions, and believe in yourself. From there, we move into action. Through this exploration, you will learn practical strategies to shift your mindset, rewrite your internal narrative, and reshape your reality. This chapter will delve into the art of storytelling and narrative psychology, understanding how the stories you tell yourself shape your perceptions, emotions, and behaviors. We will explore techniques to deconstruct the stories, identify their origins, and rewrite them to align with your aspirations and true potential.

Changing your story is not just about positive thinking. It's about positive transformation. It's about taking control of the narrative, challenging the way things have always been, and daring to chase your big dreams. It's about crafting a story of triumph, resilience, and joy for yourself. This chapter will equip you with strategies and tools to rewrite your story. You will be inspired by anecdotes of those who have successfully changed their narratives. Most importantly, you will embark on a path of personal growth and development that transcends boundaries.

THE POWER OF STORIES

Are you ready to rewrite your story? Are you prepared to transform your life? Your new story begins now, and the power lies in your hands.

Since the dawn of humanity, storytelling has been an integral part of our existence. Our ancestors gathered around fires, painted pictures on cave walls, and weaved tales transcending generations. These stories were more than mere entertainment. They were vital tools for survival. Stories have taught lessons, preserved history, and imparted wisdom.

In every culture, stories have been the bedrock of community as the thread that weaves the social fabric. From the epic sagas of ancient civilizations to the folktales whispered in the dark, stories have shaped our understanding of the world. Psychologically, storytelling is a powerful tool for making sense of the world. Stories help us process complex information, providing a framework to understand our experiences and emotions. They allow you to navigate life's chaos by offering structure and meaning. Neuroscientific research shows that when you hear stories, not only does the language processing part of your brain activate, but also those areas that would be active if you were experiencing the story's events.

In business, storytelling is used to build brands and connect with customers. The film and television industry shows the power of storytelling and shaping societal norms and expectations. Movies and TV shows not only reflect cultural values but also influence them. For instance, portraying certain professions in media can affect public perception and career aspirations. I dedicated my life to being a lawyer when I was younger because I watched all the episodes of "LA Law." Stories play a crucial role in politics and history. National narratives can shape a country's identity and values. They are always a key element in any conspiracy theory that you hear because conspiracies are often just stories being told.

Stories affect your education, your life satisfaction, and your happiness. The narratives and stories around us through media and mythology, often unnoticed, significantly shape your thoughts, behaviors, and cultural values. Of course, the media, news, advertisements, films, and social media are crucial in shaping your world understanding. And they often do it by telling you stories. This has all been proven academically. 2015 research by Kyle Hadyniak showed that newspapers historically shaped public opinion through the story, confirming that "Journalism played a major role in the deeply wounded psyche of American culture."[17] The role of newspapers in influencing public sentiment during significant historical events has always been clear.

Stories play a crucial role in preserving cultural heritage and identity. For example, indigenous cultures often use oral storytelling traditions to pass down their history, values, and beliefs. Stories have been instrumental in driving social change. The civil rights movement, for instance, used personal narratives to highlight the injustices faced by African Americans. These stories helped humanize complex social issues, mobilizing empathy and support for the movement.

Educational settings often utilize storytelling as a powerful tool for teaching. Stories can simplify complex concepts, making them more accessible and memorable for students.

For example, Jesus used parables to teach moral lessons in an engaging and relatable way. This empathetic connection makes stories so compelling and memorable on an individual level.

The stories you encounter throughout your life mold your beliefs,

---

[17] https://digitalcommons.library.umaine.edu/cgi/viewcontent.cgi?article=1218&context=honors

values, and perceptions. They can reinforce stereotypes, challenge, limit, or empower you. Collectively, stories have the power to unite or divide societies. They can be instruments of propaganda or tools for social change. The narratives a society tells itself can either uphold or question the status quo, paving the way for transformation.

The most influential stories, however, are the ones we tell ourselves.

These personal narratives are the tapestry of your experiences, beliefs, and perceptions. They are how you make sense of your past and envision your future. But often, you're unaware of the stories; they run in the background, suddenly guiding your choices and actions. Understanding these narratives is crucial because they can limit or empower you. Stories are the lens through which you see yourself and the world. Your self-perception is deeply intertwined with the narratives you hold. If your story is one of inadequacy and failure, it becomes a self-fulfilling prophecy, and you often start to live out this narrative unknowingly. On the flip side, stories of resilience and potential can propel you to great heights.

THE INFLUENCE OF NARRATIVE STRUCTURES

Are you living in a sitcom or a drama? I ask again, what sort of story are you telling yourself? Jerome Bruner, a prominent figure in psychology, developed the concept of the narrative construction of reality, which posits that human beings understand and make sense of the world primarily through stories. According to Bruner, individuals construct their identities based on narrative structures. For example, people might define themselves through a rags-to-riches story, emphasizing their journey from hardship to success. This narrative becomes a central part of their identity and influences how they perceive their life and make decisions.

Bruner argued that narrative structures influence memory. When people recall past events, they often do so in a narrative format, organizing memories to create coherent stories. This means that the way people remember events is not always a literal replay but a reconstruction based on their formed narrative. Burner's theory is evident in how teachers and students use stories to make sense of complex material in education. For instance, history teachers often present historical events as narratives with the characters' conflicts and resolutions, making the material more relatable and memorable for students.

The narrative construction of reality is also relevant in legal settings, where lawyers construct narratives to make sense of events and persuade juries. Each side in a legal case presents a story of what they believe happened. These narratives significantly influence the outcome of the case. Cultures and societies understand each other through narratives, cultural norms, values, and beliefs, which are often transmitted through stories, myths, and legends. These narratives shape how individuals within a culture perceive their world and their place within it. Don't get me started on social media. That's the new frontier in storytelling. People tell stories of themselves and the world through their social media. And it is a common element in the stories that we tell ourselves. But there is a dark side to stories that can change, manipulate, and undermine your ability to create reality.

Stories are powerful tools for communicating and understanding, but they can also be used to manipulate and deceive. This manipulation is evident in various domains, from advertising to politics. Consider storytelling in advertising campaigns that exploit emotions, creating narratives that associate happiness or success with a product, potentially leading to unrealistic expectations and consumerism. Political narratives often oversimplify super-complex issues, framing events to fit a particular agenda or using emotionally charged stories to sway public opinion. Campaigns might use stories of individual hardship or success to manipulate voters—sometimes diverting attention from systemic issues or policy details.

The ethical dimensions of storytelling are particularly crucial in media and politics, where narratives significantly impact public perception and decision-making. To combat manipulation inherent in some narratives, it's essential to develop skills for critical analysis. Always consider the source of a story and its potential motives. Analyze whether the story comes from a reputable source and what the storyteller might gain from persuading the audience. Examine the evidence supporting the narrative and look for counterarguments or alternative perspectives that might provide a more balanced view. Don't get caught up in the story; understand that you're hearing a story, not necessarily facts, even if it's factual. The fact that it is a story is important to understand. Learn to evaluate different sources' credibility and engage in exercises promoting critical thinking.

The dark side of stories reveals the potential for narratives to be used as manipulation tools and ethical breaches, especially in media and politics. But particularly in your personal story, people can tell you a story about yourself that manipulates you. Consider the story of Emma, a talented young professional. Despite her capability, she constantly told herself a story of her incompetence, a narrative stemming from a single negative experience early in her career. This narrative led her to pass up opportunities for advancement because she believed she wasn't skilled enough to succeed. Only when I got to speak with her and help reframe her narrative, highlighting her achievements and potential, did she begin to challenge her limiting story.

Then there's Alex, an aspiring entrepreneur always paralyzed by the fear of failure. His story was influenced by a family history that equated failure with disgrace, preventing him from taking risks. He would never take a risk because he was afraid of failure and the story of his family. This fear-based story held him back until he encountered a group of successful entrepreneurs who shared their stories of failure as stepping stones to success. Learning to see failure as a natural part of growth, Alex began to rewrite his story, allowing him to pursue his business aspirations.

Then, Sarah, raised in a conservative community, internalized a tale that her worth was tied to following traditional paths. This story made her suppress her true passions and interests. During college, her exposure to diverse perspectives and experiences helped her to question this story. She realized that her fear of judgment had confined her in a life that wasn't hers. She embraced her individuality by consciously rewriting her story, pursuing a career and lifestyle aligned with her true self.

My friend Sherry struggled with relationships, feeling unworthy of love due to a narrative formed from a turbulent childhood. This story led her to settle into unhealthy relationships because she believed she only deserved unhealthy relationships. That was the story that she told herself. The turning point came when she had a close friend who shared a similar background but a different self-empowerment story. Seeing another succeed despite similar beginnings inspired Sherry to rewrite her narrative, learn to value herself, and seek healthier and more fulfilling relationships.

REWRITE YOUR STORY

The process of rewriting these narratives begins with awareness. By examining your personal stories, you can identify which aspects are serving you and holding you back. The impact of stories is vast and multifaceted. Many individuals have used the power of storytelling to overcome personal challenges. For instance, someone battling addiction might find strength in narratives about recovery and redemption. The stories provide hope and a framework for understanding their journey and envisioning a path to recovery.

In therapy, storytelling can be a healing process, and patients often use narrative therapy to make sense of their experiences and emotions. Personal narratives shape how you see yourself. For example, someone who consistently tells themselves they're not good enough may struggle with low self-esteem. In contrast, a narrative centered around self-compassion and personal growth can enhance self-esteem and promote a healthier self-image. The stories people tell themselves can influence their behavior. If someone views themselves as a victim, in most situations, they might develop a passive approach to life's challenges.

Conversely, a narrative of empowerment and agency can lead to more proactive and positive behaviors. Personal narratives are crucial in the context of trauma and healing. Someone who frames a traumatic event as an insurmountable tragedy may struggle to move forward. However, reframing the narrative to focus on resilience and recovery can aid healing.

How individuals perceive their career journeys in professional settings impacts their motivation and success. A narrative of continual learning and resilience in the face of challenges can lead to greater career satisfaction and achievement. Individual narratives about social skills and the worthiness of love can significantly impact their relationships. I've often seen that if someone believes they are inherently unlikable, it can mean they face challenges creating and maintaining healthy relationships. Personal narratives can influence your health. For instance, if someone sees themselves as incapable of leading a healthy lifestyle and they tell themselves that story, they're less likely to engage in healthy behaviors. In the journey to overcome addiction, a narrative that one is perpetually helpless against addiction can hinder recovery.

Personal narratives play a significant role in mental health. The narrative of hopelessness can exacerbate depressive symptoms. The narrative of being discouraged always leads to a feeling of depression, while stories of hope and coping can alleviate them.

Often, when I meet people, I can tell right away what kind of story they're telling themselves. Some people live like they're in a sitcom. Sitcoms have historically played a role in reflecting and shaping the dynamics of the family unit. For example, the early sitcoms depicting a traditional nuclear family have transitioned to more diverse family structures, while contemporary shows mirror and influence societal changes and a progressive understanding of family dynamics. Shows like "Modern Family" challenge traditional notions of family and parenting, representing a more inclusive view of what a family can look like, thus causing a change in the world about the shape of families.

Every individual is the author of their own life story. It begins with recognizing that the power to change the narrative lies within you. Just as a caterpillar transforms into a butterfly, you can also emerge from the chrysalis of your old narratives and embrace authenticity as the cornerstone of personal transformation. Reveal your true self and let your story reflect your genuine thoughts, feelings, and aspirations, not the story others tell you. Respect and acknowledge your past without being tethered to it. Your history is not your destiny. The future is a canvas waiting for your brush, like a gardener who planted seeds with a vision of the blossoming garden and set intentions for your personal growth. What qualities do you wish to cultivate? What negative stories do you need to weed out?

Transformation is not a destination but a journey that requires persistence, patience, and a willingness to traverse the unknown. Writing is a powerful tool for self-discovery. Keep a journal to reflect on your daily thoughts and experiences that can reveal underlying narratives and stories shaping your perception that you are unaware of engaging in meditation. Journaling and meditation invite new insights and clarity, allowing you to observe your narratives from a place of detachment and objectivity.

Look for stories of people who overcome adversity by changing their narrative. Maybe it's a historical figure, a contemporary leader, or someone you know personally. Their journey can serve as a beacon illuminating the path of your transformation. Look for stories of everyday heroes who have rewritten their narratives— individuals who, despite ordinary circumstances, craft extraordinary tales of triumph from growth. Hearing and relating to the stories of others can impact your transformation process.

Let us reflect on the story of Maya, a figure whose journey of overcoming adversity by changing her narrative serves as a beacon and a fictional amalgamation that embodies the struggles and triumphs of many who have walked the path of profound change. Maya's story begins in a small, impoverished neighborhood with constant challenges and hardships. From a young age, she was told a narrative of limitation, reminding her that people from her background rarely achieved success and big dreams were a luxury she couldn't afford. Her environment reinforced this narrative, as did the low expectations set by those around her. We've seen Maya in many places. Maya's turning point came in her teenage years when she encountered a teacher who saw the potential in her that no one else did. This teacher introduces her to stories of people who had risen from similar circumstances and achieved remarkable feats. Motivated by the stories, Maya starts to rewrite her narrative. Through this work, she begins to see herself not as a victim of her circumstances but as a protagonist who can flip the script.

In her own life story, Maya pursues education with determination, studying late at night and working part-time to support her family because of the new narrative she formed. And while life is anything but smooth, she faces numerous setbacks and financial difficulties. With each challenge, Maya reinforces her new narrative of resilience and possibility. She begins to frame obstacles not as insurmountable barriers but as steps on her path to growth. Her perseverance paid off. Maya earned a scholarship to a prestigious university, the first in her family to attend college. Her academic success led her to a successful career. But more importantly, it transforms her into a role model of hope for her community. Thanks to the power of narratives, Maya shares her story and inspires others.

THE POWER OF WRITING AND REVISION

In rewriting your story, we learn to revise our own life. Neville

Goddard taught us that revision is nothing more than going back and rewriting your own story. Each moment is a brushstroke in the grand painting of your existence, but unlike a canvas, your life is not fixed. It is fluid, constantly evolving, and always open to change. At the heart of revision is the simple, profound truth that your perception of past events shapes your current reality. Every memory and experience contribute to your narrative about yourself and your life. What if the memories of these past chapters are not set in stone? What if you can revisit them not to change the events themselves but to alter your perception and emotional connection to them? Revision starts with revising past experiences, especially those that deeply impacted you. It involves seeing these events not as unchangeable truths but as scenes in a story you can reinterpret. Changing your emotional and psychological response to these past events essentially changes their influence on your current narrative.

Imagine revisiting a past event that has shaped your life. See yourself in that moment—this time, altering the script to introduce new reactions, outcomes, and emotions. Use affirmations to recast past events. Affirmations are powerful tools for rewriting the script of your memories. For example, transform a memory of failure into a lesson in resilience and strength. Rather than obsessing about all the things you did wrong in a relationship; you could choose to recount all the things you learned from the relationship and address the things you'd choose to do differently next time.

Recontextualize the emotions tied to past events. See challenging experiences as opportunities for growth and empowerment. This shift can profoundly impact your current sense of self and your future trajectory.

As you apply these principles, you see changes in your life's narrative, and opportunities arise that align more closely with your new story. Relationships evolve, and your perception of challenges transforms, seeing them not as obstacles but stepping stones to a greater purpose.

Remember, your life is a story still being written. Each day is an opportunity to revise, reshape, and move closer to the narrative you wish to live. By embracing the power of revision, you change how you view your past, live your present, and envision your future.

Rewriting is a crucial part of any writing process for authors, and their methods can be powerfully applied to rewriting your own narrative. First, by revising the opening scene, authors often revisit the opening of their stories, knowing that the beginning sets the tone for everything that follows. Writers may change the setting, introduce the key character earlier, or add a hook to better capture the reader's attention. So, reflect on the beginning of your narrative or a specific life chapter. Consider how you frame these beginnings. Are they defined by limitations or possibilities? Revising your perception of your beginnings can change how you view your journey.

Writers develop their characters, giving them depth, flaws, and growth arcs. A flat character may be rewritten to have more complex motivations or a dynamic transformation. Think of yourself as a character in your story. Have you grown and changed? Acknowledge your flaws and strengths and actively work to develop the traits that align with the person that you aspire to be.

Another thing writers use is altering the plot, akin to changing your life path. Sometimes, a story's plot doesn't flow as intended, leading authors to add twists, remove subplots, or change the story's direction to create a more compelling narrative. Consider what plot changes you could make if an aspect of your life feels stagnant or unfulfilling. Shaking things up could mean changing careers, ending toxic relationships, or starting new ventures. Like a plot twist in a novel, these changes can lead to new growth and opportunities.

Another thing writers do is change the point of view. Changing the narrator or the point of view can significantly alter a story. A tale from a different character's perspective always reveals new insights or themes as the perspective shifts. How would your story look from another person's viewpoint? This exercise can foster empathy and open your eyes to new interpretations of your experiences.

Another thing that writers do is edit the dialogue. Good dialogue is crucial for character development and plot advancement. Writers often rewrite dialogue to make it sharper, more authentic, and more impactful. Reflect on how you communicate with others. Communication with yourself is your internal and external dialogue. Evaluate if it is constructive or destructive. Improve communication, including self-talk, that can significantly alter your narrative.

Adding descriptive details is another way authors enrich their writing experience. Details bring a story to life. Writers add sensory descriptions or emotional nuances to enrich the readers' experience. Pay more attention to the details of your daily life. Appreciate the small moments, the textures of your experiences, and the emotions they evoke. This heightened awareness can add depth and richness to your life story.

You can also cut out unnecessary parts of your story. Authors always like to kill their darlings to remove parts of their story that don't serve the overall narrative, no matter how well loved. Identify aspects of your life that no longer serve your habits, beliefs, or relationships. Letting go of these can streamline your narrative, making room for elements that better serve your current and future chapters.

MOVIE STORY FORMULAS

Another aspect of stories that must be explored is the story formulas, structure, and pattern. Understanding these frameworks can help you recognize the underlying pattern in your personal story, enabling you to reframe and reshape them more effectively. I found it fascinating when I became a screenwriter and understood how stories were structured. After that, I could watch a movie and see the structure and skeleton of the story. The most popular formula is the hero's journey. This structure involves stages like the call to adventure, trials, tribulations, and the return. The hero's journey is useful for viewing life as a process of transformation and self-discovery.

Then there's the three-act structure. Many stories are created in the structure, a foundational narrative form in literature and film, comprising the setup establishing characters in the conflict. Then there's the confrontation, facing and managing the conflict, and resolving the conflict in life. These acts are a progression of challenges you face, how you deal with them, and their eventual resolution.

Another classic structure is the Cinderella arc, a rags-to-riches story where the protagonist overcomes oppressive circumstances to achieve a significant transformation, often found in fairy tales and success stories. This arc can reflect personal narratives of overcoming adversity and achieving significant life changes.

Other modern story structures are overcoming the monster, a story of battling and overcoming a formidable adversary—often external but sometimes internal. In real life, this could relate to facing fears, addictions, or overcoming a significant life challenge. Review your life and decide if it's a tragedy or a comedy. Tragic patterns follow the protagonist's fall due to a fatal flaw or mistake. Comedic patterns often involve a lighter, more humorous approach to life challenges. These patterns can reflect periods of struggle or joy in your life and affect your attitude and choices or impact your outcomes.

By understanding these various story formulas, structures, and patterns, you can gain insight into the narrative of your own life. You can identify which patterns you are living and consider if they are serving you well or if you need to embark on a new narrative path.

AFFIRMATIONS—WHAT STORY ARE YOU TELLING YOURSELF

If you want to change your story, use these affirmations as a jumping-off point to begin changing your narrative. Say these with me.

- I am the author of my story, and every day, I write a new page filled with strength and purpose.

- I tell my story with courage and optimism, knowing each word reflects my strength and resilience.

- I write my future intentionally and clearly, focusing on my goals and dreams with unwavering dedication.

- I write my interactions with love and respect, fostering relationships that bring joy and fulfillment.

- I write my successes as milestones, celebrating each achievement as a testament to my capabilities.

- I write my passions as the driving force of my narrative, allowing them to guide and inspire my journey.

- I write my moments of stillness as crucial scenes. Understanding that reflection and rest are critical to a balanced life.

- I change my story from one of doubt to one of confidence and self-belief.

- I change my story to focus on gratitude—appreciating every experience that shapes me.

- I change my story to highlight resilience in the face of adversity.

- I change my story to be a journey of discovery, exploring new aspects of myself and the world around me.

- I change my story from a narrative of victimhood to one of empowerment and agency.

- I change my story to include forgiveness—both of myself and others—as a path to healing and peace.

- In every chapter, I change my story to embrace each

moment as a gift and an opportunity to learn.

- I change my story to inspire others, proving that change and growth are always possible.

So my question to you is, what story are you telling yourself?

Now's the time to change it. Write your story of success, love, happiness, joy, and fulfillment so you can expect the best in every moment.

CHAPTER ELEVEN

THE ART OF EXPECTATION

"We tend to get what we expect."

—*Norman Vincent Peale*

In the exhilarating landscape of human consciousness, where thoughts weave the fabric of your reality, there exists a powerful yet often overlooked element: expectation. The art of expectation delves into the profound influence that your anticipations, hopes, and fears have on the tapestry of your life. It's a voyage into the heart of how you shape your reality through the lens of your perceptions and beliefs. Your expectations are not mere passive predictions but active creators in the theater of your existence. Expectations sculpt your experience, color your interactions, and, in many ways, dictate the narrative of your personal and collective saga.

This chapter seeks to unravel this intricate web, guiding you through a transformative understanding of how expectations can be harnessed as a tool for growth, joy, and fulfillment.

Expectations, when approached with awareness and balance, can become a catalyst for profound change. They can elevate your experience, enrich your relationships, and empower your aspirations. Yet, when left unchecked, they can also lead you to a labyrinth of disappointments and unmet desires. Understanding this dual nature is critical. This chapter's narrative is more than just a guide. It's an invitation to a paradigm shift, a re-envisioning of how you interact with your innermost desires and fears. Through a blend of philosophical insight and practical wisdom, I offer you a roadmap for navigating the delicate balance of aspiring and surrendering, dreaming and doing, expecting, and accepting.

How can you master the art of expectation and transform it from a subconscious undercurrent into a conscious, powerful tool for crafting your reality? The path ahead is rich with potential and discovery, a testament to the limitless possibilities that await when you learn to harness the true power of your expectations. Right now, in this moment, you stand on the brink of a vast ocean of possibilities. Each wave has a different future, and each ripple has an unexplored potential. This is where expectation plays its part, not as a passive onlooker but as the wind guiding the waves. You are not merely wishing upon a star but aligning the cosmos to your will. Expectation is the architect of your experience. It's an invisible energy, a silent language spoken by your innermost self to the universe.

When you expect greatness, you don't just attract opportunities; you create them and become a magnet for abundance, joy, and fulfillment. I'm not talking just about optimism but about a fundamental principle of life that is as real as gravity. Expect the best, and the universe will conspire to meet your vision. Open your heart and mind. The world you desire is not just a dream. It's an expectation waiting to be realized.

REALIZE YOUR IDEAL FUTURE

Several years ago, I found myself at a crossroads. Life had thrown its share of challenges my way. My career felt stagnant. My relationships were strained, and I was not fulfilled. Each day felt like a repetition of the last, devoid of excitement or purpose. It was during this period that I stumbled upon the concept of positive expectation. And though initially I was skeptical, one evening, as I sat pondering my situation, I made a decision. In the past, I had constantly dwelled on what was going wrong. I chose to expect things to go right. Aligning with this decision was not an easy shift. Doubts and fears had always been my constant companion for so long. They were a part of me, perhaps a whisper of my inner self. But my inner self urged me to trust in the power of expectation. I began visualizing my ideal future, which offered growth, creativity, love, and fulfillment.

Each morning, I'd wake up and spend a couple of minutes expecting success. I would see myself thriving in my dream job. I didn't know how it would happen, but I trusted the process. Slowly, things started to change for me. Opportunities I never imagined began to present themselves, and a chance encounter led to a conversation that became a wonderful opportunity for me. It was as if the universe was rearranging itself to align with my expectations. I didn't stop there; my relationships improved as I started to expect the best from them. I approached interactions with positivity and openness, which was often reciprocated. I expected good things from people, I expected people to be good, and life began to feel vibrant and filled with possibilities previously obscured by my negative mindset of expecting the worst.

This practice taught me that our expectations are not just idle daydreams. They're powerful signals that we send out to the world, and more often than not, the world responds in kind. By expecting the best, I unknowingly opened the door to a life that was richer, more fulfilling, and aligned with my deepest desires. This transformation was nothing short of miraculous. It has shown me that when we shift our focus from doubt to anticipation of good, we don't just change our outlook; we change our reality.

I want that for you.

I had a friend whose most cherished possession was a small piece of land behind her little cottage, which she transformed into a luscious garden. This garden was not just a patch of earth where plants grew—it was a symbol of her belief in the power of expectation. One spring, there was a terrible drought. The fields lay barren, and the hearts of her friends and family were heavy with despair. She, however, planted her seeds as she did every year and expected a bountiful garden. Her friends and people in the city scoffed at her, asking, "Why waste your time? Can't you see the land is too dry?" She would smile and say, "I choose to expect the best. My garden will grow."

I saw her tend her garden and water the seeds with the little water she had, always maintaining a positive outlook. She spoke to her plants, encouraging them to grow and expecting them to thrive despite the circumstances. As weeks passed, something miraculous happened. Tiny green shoots began to sprout in her garden. Everyone she knew was astounded. None of their gardens had shown any signs of life, yet hers was coming alive. When I asked her how she could grow this garden during such a drought, she said it was about the power of positive expectation.

EMBRACE THE ENERGY OF EXPECTATION

When we expect good things to happen, we open ourselves up to possibilities and attract positive energy and outcomes—even in the hardest times. Expectation is a subtle yet profound force. It is an invisible energy often overlooked. It is as real and potent as the wind that bends the willow or the tide that shapes the shore. To understand expectation is to hold the key to a hidden realm where thoughts are the architects of your reality. Expectation, in its purest form, is akin to a seed planted in the fertile soil of your mind. It is nurtured by belief, watered by conviction, and brought to life by the sunlight of your attention. What we expect with certainty, we summon in our experience as surely as the dawn follows the night.

How does expectation influence your actions, your relationships, and the unfolding events of your existence? In what way does expectation shape your perceptions of color and your experiences and dictate the boundaries of your potential? The science of expectation is deeply rooted in psychological principles. Research in the field of cognitive psychology has shown that expectations can significantly influence both perceptions and behavior. A seminal study by Rosenthal and Jacobson in 1968, often referred to as the Pygmalion effect, demonstrated how teachers' expectations of their students' intellectual abilities influenced the students' performance.[18] This phenomenon, also known as a self-fulfilling prophecy, underlies the power of expectation in shaping outcomes. Further supporting this, studies in the realm of neuroscience have illustrated how expectations can alter brain activity and research on pain perception. For instance, the expectation of relief has been shown to activate endogenous

---

[18] https://link.springer.com/article/10.1007/BF02322211

opioid systems in the brain, thereby reducing pain, according to Ben Gao in 2011.[19] These studies indicate that expectation can have a direct physiological impact.

Historically, the concept of expectation has been intertwined with cultural and philosophical thought. Ancient philosophies such as stoicism emphasize the importance of managing expectations to achieve a state of tranquility. The Stoics believed that uncontrolled expectations could lead to emotional disturbances. In Eastern philosophies, particularly within Buddhism, there is an emphasis on the nature of expectation and its impact on human suffering. The concept of dukkha in Buddhism, often translated as suffering or dissatisfaction, is partly attributed to the gap between reality and human expectations. The teaching suggests that understanding and managing these expectations is the key to reducing suffering. So, on the one hand, we have expectations as this powerful force that can create your reality. Yet, on the other hand, in Buddhism and Eastern texts and stoicism, we are told it can lead to suffering.

Cultural perspectives also play a significant role in shaping expectations. Hofstede's cultural dimensions theory, in 1980, illustrated how culture influences values and expectations within societies.[20] For instance, individualistic cultures tend to emphasize personal achievement and expectations more than collectivist cultures, which focus more on communal goals and expectations. The science and philosophy of expectation encompasses a broad spectrum, from psychological and physiological impacts to cultural and philosophical interpretations. Understanding these foundations leads to comprehending how expectations shape

---

[19] https://www.ncbi.nlm.nih.gov/pmc/articles/PMC4464817/

[20] https://doi.org/10.1177/0022022118798505

your perceptions, influence your behaviors, and ultimately craft your reality.

When you expect with a deep sense of certainty, you're not just hoping you are creating. You are aligning your vibration with the desired outcome, tuning your frequency to the possibility you wish to manifest. It's as if you're whispering to the universe, guiding it toward the reality you yearn to experience. This notion is reflected in many spiritual traditions, or the power of belief and thought is recognized as a potent force in shaping your destiny. In this view, the mind is not confined within your skull. It extends its influence far beyond the world through the vibrations of expectation.

But here's a delightful paradox. While we shape our reality with our expectations, we must also surrender to the flow of the universe. It is a delicate balance between intention and letting go, between directing your energy and being open to the myriad ways the universe can respond.

In this interplay of expectation and reality, where thoughts ripple across the vastness of existence, you find yourself a participant in this cosmic dance. Each expectation you hold is like a note in an infinite symphony, contributing to the creation of a harmonious or sometimes discordant melody. This melody is your life, your reality continuously shaped and reshaped by the vibrations of your deepest anticipations. I love to refer to this as the eternal cosmic dance and the infinite symphony. The reason I do this is that it's so accurate. Your expectations emit a unique frequency, a vibration that resonates. These vibrations are not isolated. They interact with the energies of others in the world. But the universe at large is a magnificent web of interconnectedness, a tapestry of energy, where every thread is interwoven with countless others.

Your expectations are not merely passive wishes cast into the void. They are active dynamic forces engaging with the energies around you. When you expect with intention, belief, and emotion, you're not just hoping for a certain outcome. You're energetically aligning yourself with it. You become attuned to the frequency of your desired reality, and in doing so, you invite it into your experience. But there is an art to this alignment, a wisdom in understanding the flow of these energies. It is not about imposing your will upon the universe. It's about harmonizing with it. Like a leaf floating on a stream, you set your course but remain open to the meanderings of the current. Your expectations, while directed, are also flexible, adapting to the ever-changing flow of the universe. The boundary between you as the observer and the observed blurs. You are not separate from the reality you experience; you are intimately connected to it, a co-creator in its manifestation.

Your thoughts and expectations are not confined to the realm of the mind. They are extensions of your being, reaching out and shaping the fabric of reality. Reality is a reflection of your inner state, a mirror of your expectations. In all its complexity and wonder, the external world is a canvas upon which your internal vibrations paint their picture. By mastering the art of expectation and tuning your vibration to the frequency of your highest aspiration, you learn to compose a reality that resonates with your soul's deepest desires.

The quality of your expectations determines the quality of your actions. High expectations can lead to higher efforts and aspirations, leading you to drive and push beyond your perceived limits. Rhonda Byrne, the writer of "The Secret," says, "Expectation is a powerful attractive force. Expect the things you want and don't expect the things you don't want." Brian Tracy, one of my favorite authors, also says, "Whatever we expect with confidence becomes our own self-fulfilling prophecy." Tracy's observation speaks to the self-fulfilling nature of your expectations. When you expect something with confidence, you subconsciously set in motion a series of thoughts and actions that can make that expectation a reality.

THE FLOW OF SYNCHRONICITY

In understanding the art of expectation, synchronicity and flow become your guiding star, where the universe whispers secrets in a language understood only by those attuned to its frequency. Synchronicity in the realm of manifestation is akin to cosmic poetry in motion. It's the universe's way of nodding in agreement and showing that you are in harmony with its infinite rhythms. So, you must observe the coincidences and patterns in your life. They're not mere accidents but the universe's language. Learn to read the signs, interpret their meanings, and understand your expectations.

Live each day with intention, and when clear intentions drive your actions, synchronicities become more apparent, guiding you toward your goals. Then, you can manifest through flow, engaging in activities that ignite your passion. When you do what you love, entering a state of flow becomes natural. You create an inviting moment that supports concentration and focus. Distractions are the enemies of flow. I mentioned flow because one of the hardest things is overcoming challenges, setbacks, and unrealized expectations; as the Buddha says, it is the cause of all suffering. My argument to you is that this does not mean that you should expect nothing.

Challenges and setbacks are not mere obstacles. They are catalysts for growth; you're not trying to avoid them. They are invitations to rise to your fullest potential, and encountering them doesn't mean that what you're expecting will not happen. It's a fundamental truth that the path to success is always paved with trials and tribulations. Yet it is in the heart of these challenges that you discover your true strength and resilience.

The key lies in your response to disappointment in your ability to adjust your expectations without losing sight of your goals. If you continually assume that everything is working to your advantage, that something wonderful is about to happen for you, it allows you to deal with disappointment and adjust your expectations. Disappointment is an inevitable companion on the road to achieving your wish fulfilled. It tests your resolve, challenges your expectations, and often requires a recalibration of your goals. However, it's crucial to understand that adjusting expectations isn't about lowering your standard or conceding defeat.

It's about intelligently reevaluating your strategies and finding new, more effective paths to your objectives. So, view each disappointment not as a failure of expectation but as a learning opportunity. Ask yourself, "What can I learn from this experience? How can it make me better?" Keep your disappointment in perspective. Remember, a setback is just a moment in time, not the entirety of your journey. Fine-tune your expectations and strategies in response to setbacks. Be flexible in your approach but steadfast in your pursuit of excellence.

Resilience is the cornerstone of overcoming challenges. Thus, resilience is one of the keys to the art of expectation. It's the ability to bounce back from setbacks to face adversity with courage and determination. Resilience is not an innate trait but a skill that can be developed. So, foster an attitude of optimism and hope. Believe in your ability to overcome challenges. Surround yourself with people who uplift and support you. That strong network of friends and family mentors can be a powerful source of strength in tough times.

Every setback carries with it the seeds of wisdom and growth. Minding these insights and using them to propel yourself forward is the key. Reflect on your experiences, identify what went wrong, and develop strategies to avoid similar pitfalls in the future. Don't let setbacks be a self-fulfilling prophecy that defines your future expectations. Take a step back and objectively analyze your setbacks. Identify the factors that contributed to the outcome. Based on your analysis, develop new strategies to tackle your goals. Continue to expect the best, be innovative, and be open to new approaches. Put the insights you gain into action and use them to strengthen your resolve and refine your path to success.

Overcoming challenges and setbacks is an integral part of the journey towards greatness. It requires dealing with disappointment with grace, building resilience against adversity, and learning from each experience. Remember, every challenge you face is an opportunity to grow stronger, wiser, and more capable. Embrace difficult moments that shape your character and develop the fortitude needed to achieve extraordinary success.

EXCESS POTENTIAL

One of the most important aspects of the art of expectation is about managing your expectations to align with the desired outcomes while avoiding the creation of excess potential—a term used to describe the imbalances caused by overly intense emotions or attachments to specific results. You have most assuredly seen this. People get caught up in something they want and desperately crave, placing excess importance upon it, which is what makes it so that it doesn't happen. Expectations are not just passive hopes or fears about what might happen. They are active forces that shape the reality around you.

Shaping of reality is not straightforward. When our expectations are too intense or charged with strong emotions, whether positive or negative, they create excess potential. This excess potential is believed to disturb the balance of the surrounding energy field, leading to unintended and often undesirable outcomes. The art then lies in maintaining a state of balanced expectation where you are neither overly attached to nor completely detached from the outcome. This is akin to walking a tightrope between caring too much and not caring at all. The key is to desire and envision a positive outcome while simultaneously accepting any possibility.

This acceptance creates a state of inner harmony and balance, reducing the likelihood of generating excess potential. In practice, this means setting intentions and goals while remaining open to the multitude of ways these goals can manifest. And they, in many cases, can manifest by experiencing obstacles, delays, and setbacks. So, this suggests a focus on the process rather than the outcome, enjoying the journey, engaging in actions for your own sake, and finding value in the experience itself. Regardless of the result, there are ways to practice this art of balanced expectation. This approach aligns with the idea of letting go of the need for specific outcomes and thus minimizing the creation of excess potential.

The art of expectation is about cultivating a balanced state of mind where desires and goals are pursued without intense emotional attachments. You can have intense emotions about the end in which you're moving towards but not be attached to the outcome. This balanced state aligns more harmoniously with the desired outcomes and ensures a smoother journey by avoiding the pitfalls of excess potential.

Buddha taught that expectations are like shadows. They follow us, often unseen and unacknowledged, profoundly shaping our journey, often leading to suffering. I contend that suffering happens when you attach importance to desired specific outcomes. So, as the Buddha does, I advise you to observe your expectations with a gentle curiosity. Be like a sage sitting by the river watching your thoughts and expectations flow by; don't cling to them, and do not resist them. In this way, you allow the river of life to find its natural course.

Some expectations can arise from your deepest desires and fears. They are the mind's way of attempting to assert control over what some say is uncontrollable. And while I'm saying that the way your life unfolds is controllable, it is an art that continually evolves as the flowing river of life. By acknowledging this fluidity, you can learn to let go of the rigid structures that you build in your mind so you can flow with life—embracing its unpredictability with grace and equanimity. In this graceful surrender, you will find a profound freedom.

How do we implement the art of expectation by reducing importance? Suppose that you're aiming for a promotion at work. Instead of obsessing over the outcome, visualize yourself in the desired position and cultivate a sense of detachment. Acknowledge that while this is what you want, your happiness and self-worth are not solely dependent on achieving it.

If you're working on a personal project, like writing a book, focus on the joy and fulfillment that comes from the writing process itself and enjoy the act of creating the book rather than fixating solely on the end goal of publication or recognition.

When planning a vacation, instead of setting high expectations for every detail to be perfect, maintain a positive yet neutral outlook and expect to enjoy the trip. However, be open to the experiences as they come, whether they align with your initial plans or not.

If you're trying to sell your house, rather than pinning all your hopes on one perfect buyer, offering your dream price, remain open to different selling possibilities. This might mean considering various types of offers or being open to adjusting your expectations based on market feedback.

In relationships, instead of expecting your partner to fulfill every need or match every ideal, appreciate them for who they are. Reduce the emotional charge around expectations by focusing on mutual understanding and growth.

Suppose you're working on improving your health, setting goals for exercise and diet, and practicing acceptance of your body's responses. In that case, your focus should be on healthy practices rather than being overly fixated on specific weight or fitness milestones.

When attending a social event, enjoy the experience rather than trying to control every aspect of the interaction. This could mean engaging in conversations and activities that arise naturally rather than trying to steer everything according to your preconceived expectations.

Aim for advancement and success while cultivating a sense of contentment in your present career. This balance can help reduce the pressure and anxiety often accompanying professional aspirations.

THE ROLE OF FAITH

The Bible provides guidance on the art of expectation. John 14:1 asserts,

"Let not your heart be troubled; you believe in God, believe also in Me."

Expectation, in its truest form, is a form of faith. It is the assurance of things hoped for, the conviction of things not seen, just as the scripture says. Hebrews 11:1 reminds us, "Now faith is the substance of things hoped for, the evidence of things not seen." When you expect with conviction, you're activating the creative power of your imagination, aligning your inner vision with the external manifestation of your desires.

Consider the story of the woman with the issue of blood in the gospels. She had suffered for 12 long years. Her expectation of healing was so strong that she believed she would be made whole if only she could touch the hem of Jesus' garment. And so, it was her expectation fueled by unwavering faith that brought forth her healing. The story is not just a testament to physical healing but a powerful illustration of the principle that our expectations, when imbued with faith, become the vessels through which miracles flow.

AFFIRMATIONS—THE ART OF EXPECTATION

As you are deeply connected with the power of expectation, repeat these affirmations in your mind or out loud, feeling their truth resonating within you.

- I am aligned with the frequency of positive expectations.

- I expect great things and attract them effortlessly.

- Every day, I expect and welcome happiness, health, and prosperity with open arms.

- I am confident in my future as my expectations of success and joy are coming to fruition.

- I expect miracles, and they manifest in my life.

- I expect to meet the right people and find the right opportunities at the perfect time.

- My expectation of abundance and joy attracts them to me effortlessly.

- My mind is a beacon of hope and expectation; it lights the path to a bright and successful future.

- I expect my journey to be filled with abundant blessings and remarkable experiences.

- I expect to find beauty and positivity in every moment and in every situation.

- I expect my relationships to be enriching, supportive, and full of love.

- I expect to continually evolve, learn, and thrive in all aspects of my life.

- I expect my actions to lead to positive outcomes and rewarding experiences.

- I expect to find peace within myself and spread it to the world around me.

- I expect every setback to pave the way for a greater comeback.

Allow these affirmations to resonate deeply within you and allow your connection to this frequency of positive expectation to grow. Understanding that expectation is an art in avoiding excess potential, placing too much importance on any given expectation.

When unrealized expectations occur, simply look at them as wonderful opportunities to learn and grow. So go out into the world, continue to expect the very best and remember that whatever happens, every day is a second chance to try again.

CHAPTER TWELVE

EVERY DAY IS A SECOND CHANCE

"Tomorrow when I awaken, the slate will be clean, and a new day will stretch before me."

— *Lori Hatcher*

In activating your power, you must understand the power of second chances. No matter what happened yesterday, today is a new day. Every day is a second chance. It's a profound truth you must become aware of. When I look back on my life, I have had the very worst days, and the most horrible things have happened, yet all was resolved the very next day. I stay open to each day as being full of infinite possibilities. The day after I was shot, a story I talked about in my first book, I awoke the next day with the profound realization that every day is a second chance.

Remember that in the quiet hours of the morning, when the world is still asleep, and the stars haven't yet given way to the sun, there lies this profound truth: no matter what you're going through, no matter what you have encountered, and no matter how bad it seems right now, every day is a second chance.

There's a gentle whisper if you listen for it; in the heart of every awakening soul—every day is a second chance. This simple yet profound realization is the cornerstone of your journey toward inner peace, transformation, and the reality you wish to create. It's a journey that transcends time and space, rooted deeply in the wisdom of ages and the personal stories of those who have walked this path before us.

This ancient wisdom echoes the universal truth: every sunrise brings a new opportunity for change, forgiveness, and growth. Lamentations 3:22-23 confirms, "The steadfast love of the LORD never ceases; his mercies never come to an end; they are new every morning; great is your faithfulness."

Buddha said, "Every morning, we are born again. What we do today is what matters most." Just like the sun rises each morning, we, too, can rise and shine to create light after a period of darkness.

Someone very close to me spent her days working in shipping and receiving at Target. She was talented and passionate and dreamed of creating and being creative. She made everything beautiful around her. She could take the smallest object and turn it into something beautiful. But she wasn't aware of that power and inspiration deep within her. There was this great desire to be an artist, to create, and to be successful. Her fear of rejection kept her desires hidden from the world. Being an artist was always a dream in the back of her mind, something unattainable that would never happen for her. She had to take care of her kids and work all the time, barely scraping by.

One day, wandering the city, she stumbled upon a street fair filled with artists showcasing their work, and she was mesmerized by the vibrant array of paintings, sculptures, and crafts. Amidst the creativity, she met an elderly artist whose eyes sparkled with wisdom, and he noticed her interest and started a conversation. She shared her passion that she could one day paint like him, but also her fear of not being good enough. This man listened intently, smiled gently, and said, "Every day is a second chance. Each morning, the sun rises. Don't let the setbacks of yesterday dim the potential of today." His sentiment struck a chord with her, and she realized that every day she chose not to share her art, she missed an opportunity to grow, learn, and possibly succeed.

After that chance meeting, she started to paint and learned how to paint by watching YouTube videos and taking classes when she could afford it. Still struggling financially, she gathered the courage, and her best paintings began to sell. With trembling hands, she set up her small little website and started to sell these paintings. The last time I spoke with her, she'd sold over 2000 paintings! To her surprise, people stopped, admired, and bought her paintings. Each day presents a brand new opportunity. After giving up on her dreams and bringing them to fruition, she always remembers every day is a second chance.

In the Bible, we find countless stories of redemption and second chances. Jonah, who fled from God's call, was given another opportunity to fulfill His purpose. Peter, who denied Christ three times, was entrusted with the keys to the kingdom. These biblical stories are not just historical accounts. They are reminders that no matter how far we stray, there's always a path back, a new chapter waiting to be written.

Each day heralds a new beginning; the power of your belief and imagination plays a pivotal role. It is through these faculties that you can reshape your reality. Turning the dreams of today into the lived experiences of tomorrow.

AFFIRMATIONS—EVERY DAY IS A SECOND CHANCE

You can say these affirmations to affirm your understanding of renewal and the second chance that you've been given at this very moment.

- Every day is a new opportunity to start over and make a positive change.

- I am grateful for second chances and embrace them with an open heart.

- I allow myself the grace to begin anew and rewrite my story.

- With each sunrise, I am reborn, ready to tackle the world with fresh eyes.

- I release my past mistakes and welcome the chance to grow and learn.

- I am deserving of second chances and use them to better myself.

- I trust in the power of renewal and believe in my ability to change.

- Every moment is a chance to turn it all around, and I seize this moment with courage.

- I am resilient and capable of bouncing back stronger with each new opportunity.

- I celebrate the gift of today, knowing It's my chance to create a brighter tomorrow.

- I am not defined by my past. I am shaped by my present actions and choices.

- Today, I choose to let go of old patterns and embrace new possibilities.

- I am empowered to take bold steps forward, knowing every day has a chance to evolve.

- I welcome the opportunity to rebuild and transform my life starting now.

- My potential is limitless, and I am ready to explore new paths on this journey.

Go out into this day knowing it is a new and wonderful day and that every day is a second chance to activate your unlimited power.

CHAPTER THIRTEEN

ACTIVATE YOUR POWER

"Power is not given to you. You have to take it."

— *Beyoncé Knowles*

This final chapter is an activation designed for you to discover and increase your unlimited and innate power. After completing this chapter, you will find your subconscious mind reprogrammed and your life changed with an awareness of increased power.

ACTIVATE YOUR POWER

As these words flow you begin to feel your breath deepen into a slow, steady rhythm. All tensions ease from your shoulders. While mindfulness takes root for the journey ahead, beginning in this nurturing space is essential—a sanctuary where inner wisdom may awaken. I am your guide for exploring the innate power source lying dormant within. By cultivating empowered perspectives and habits of thought, you will lift away all perceived restrictions on your potential. No longer must life's circumstances dictate your experience of reality. Together, through this unknowing hypnosis, you will discover the strength and capabilities available when you believe fully in yourself. You feel deeply settled now as our exploration begins.

The purpose of the journey is to cultivate a mindset where you perceive yourself as the author of your reality rather than a victim of outside forces. Through scientific studies, we know our thinking patterns directly impact life's outcomes. Research in neuroscience, epigenetics, and positive psychology consistently show a link between the stories we tell ourselves and our experiences. Your very biology responds to the worlds your mind creates. What you focus on grows. Regular perceptions of limits only erect those exact boundaries in physical reality. On the contrary, minds open to endless possibilities manifest circumstances reflecting that expansive viewpoint. Hence, cultivating an empowerment mindset helps ensure life events align with your highest intentions and values.

With each word and empowered outlook, you are capable of dissolving life's stickiest traps. I'm sure you've had those times when negative thought loops grip tight, and you're repeating mantras of doubt. "I can't," "It's impossible," "Who am I to believe in myself?"

Let us now take a few moments to allow the body to relax deeply so the mind may open like a flower. Begin by slowly bringing awareness to any tension in the hands and forearms. Without effort, allow those muscles to soften and release. Feel the relaxation spreading gently up each arm into the shoulders, neck, jaw, face, and eyes. Turn awareness within as leaves fall from trees in your mind's eye. Visualize each worry and each ingrained limitation of fear released on the breeze, like crumpled leaves drifting out of reach. See them flutter briefly before dissolving. With each breath, feel calm, feeling like a gracefully standing tree branch, poised for what comes next without clinging to what once was. Stay in this peaceful state of release for as long as you choose, knowing worries have loosened their grip for now. When ready, bring awareness back to the surrounding tranquility with gratitude for this respite from mental noise. Emerging to the present moment, see if you can maintain the calm again.

Now is the time to foster the expansion of your power to gently encourage cultivating a vision of your innate potential without limitations. Think of yourself like a seed that has lain dormant too long yet contains a vastness of life within its tiny form, just waiting for the right conditions to unfold. Perhaps you've lived as if confined to a narrow identity imposed by old beliefs, habits, or circumstances. I invite you now to sense deeper truths below surface perceptions to feel stirring power within an unbounded essence that knows any restrictions, like a seed absorbing warmth in rains of change, open to possibilities beyond what you have seen your shape to be.

Have faith that conditions nurture hidden strengths and creativity into fullness. Just as sunlight coaxes tender shoots from simple shells, for now, trust the simple truth that within lies a creative force desiring expression. All you need to do is gently remove whatever obscures its light. See yourself capable of so much growth, with incredible potential for beauty and contribution waiting in the wings of your being. Stay centered here. Let this empowered vision take root and spread quietly through every part of you.

With care and understanding for yourself, reflect for a moment on how long-held beliefs or internal narratives may subtly influence your life experience for better or worse. This powerful evolution will unfold gently each day. Thank you for opening your mind to its potential and committing to this inner work. Understanding comes slowly but surely as we make space for more profound knowing. For now, see if you can maintain mindfulness of this empowered perspective as you go about daily activities.

Let the healing waters of awareness gently carry away rigid assumptions as the coming tide smooths the shoreline. Your inner freedom begins.

Now, try shifting your perspective through visualization. Recall a difficult memory where self-criticism ruled your inner dialogue, perhaps when you felt afraid or anxious or that you had failed. Bring the scene softly to mind by observing from a distance first so any residual intensity can fade. Now imagine walking into the memory, approaching your past self who is suffering with compassion, and sharing words of reassurance, understanding, and hope that all will be well. There are lessons to learn, even from perceived mistakes. If resistance arises when viewing the memory, such as thoughts of "I can't do this" and/or "It won't make a difference," acknowledge and let them go with patience. We all have a deeper knowing within that can replace limiting patterns once given permission, staying present with breath and sensations.

Imagine your past self, gradually relaxing as tension releases from the body. Envision exchanging harshness for supportiveness by retelling the story from this more empathic understanding. Keep visualizing this exchange until the image feels complete. How does it feel to hold yourself with care, even in struggle? Your true nature desires growth, not self-punishment. This small act of kindness can ripple outward to reshape future dialogue and choice.

THOUGHTS ARE EMERGING STATES

Do your thoughts empower you or hold you back from your highest self?

Now, experiment—consciously flexing your viewpoints around these patterns of thought. Notice how changing words like "failure" to "learning opportunity" alter your emotional and physical state. Bring to mind challenging circumstances from a place of compassionate curiosity instead of harsh judgment. What possibilities or alternatives emerge? Dialogue with yourself as if speaking to a loved one. Communicate encouragement where you used to criticize, which widens your perceptual lens to see beyond old mental habits. Commit fully to this perspective and work through gentle self-observation. Transformation happens one insight at a time, and each chosen affirmation moves you closer to realizing your inherent power. Progress may seem slow, so always stay determined and patient with yourself.

Let's now guide a visualization of shifting inner perspectives. Bring your awareness inward to notice any recurrent self-doubt, shame, or judgment. It may relate to an aspect of yourself, relationships, or situations in life. Generally observed without harshness, the negative thought patterns surrounding the shame might hear repetitive phrases about not measuring up or being unworthy. Now, envision walking into this cyclic mental conversation and stopping the words with breath and presence. As your inner critic quiets, feel openness arise inside. Say new empowering statements about your inherent worth, courage, or ability to connect with others through empathy and care from this place.

Affirm your basic goodness just as you are. These positive

declarations will guide you as you reimagine past scenarios through kinder eyes. Notice how personas and interactions shift profoundly without judgment. All people have layered depths, and no single event defines another's or one's character. Stay with this liberating perspective as long as it feels supportive. But it nurtures self-acceptance from within and outward. You possess innate gifts to offer this world by living authentically according to your heart. This practice cultivates peaceful empowerment for all your relationships.

To reinforce these techniques, reflect on a recent mild frustration or annoyance. Perhaps a brief interchange that left you feeling irritated. Bring the memory to mind and experiment with revising your internal dialogue around the event. Notice the subtle yet impactful difference choosing alternative viewpoints makes to your state of being. By exercising flexibility—even around ordinary frustrations, you open to inner and outer flow while cultivating empathy, optimism, and resilience as a way of being. I encourage you to remain attentive to lifelong patterns seeking transformation. Notice mindsets needing flexibility, and practice consciously choosing alternative viewpoints daily for liberating insight and well-being.

As you read my words, allow yourself to soften while maintaining an open awareness and being receptive to suggestions. It's centered on your inner authority. Visualize a thriving landscape of your ideal future brimming with promise, possibility and power. See yourself embodying life from a successful vantage, appreciate each sensory detail, from colors richer to smiles wider, peace more profound. Breathe in fully this altered condition. With exhalation, any resistance or disbelief in manifesting such renewal is released.

You sculpt your world through the words you speak into being. Discover this inner power now. Roam this landscape, interacting freely within your ideal reality. How do responsibilities appear lighter when approached with affirming mindsets? Notice how supportive others are in their interactions with this newly potent version of you. Feel deeply the emotions this future elicits: appreciation, empowerment, joy, and contribution. Sow entirely in these feelings that you truly experience and believe in this as your current, ever-increasing reality.

AFFIRMATIONS—ACTIVATE YOUR POWER

Have faith in your ability to shape challenging moments by reshaping thought patterns and beliefs through words, transforming latent into manifested power. Allow this power to blossom abundantly and fully support your affirmative journey. The previous paragraphs have been designed to pull you into an open state in which you can say the following affirmations that will release your complete power.

- I am powerful.

- The infinite intelligence within me knows no obstacles.

- Every step I take is guided toward greater power and achievement.

- I am surrounded by the boundless energy of the universe, which empowers me to manifest my deepest desires and dreams.

- With every breath, I inhale power and exhale any feelings of limitation.

- My mind is a fertile garden where the seeds of success, power, and prosperity grow abundantly, nurtured by unwavering faith and positive actions.

- I am so happy and grateful now that large sums of power come to me, easily and quickly, in increasing quantities, from multiple sources, on a continuous basis, in the best interest of all, with the free will of all, that I get to use joyfully.

- In moments of decision, I tap into this reservoir of power.

- The door to my greatest potential power is now unlocked. I now open it.

- My path to power is clear, and my outcomes are successful.

- I am a magnet for power.

- My life reflects my thoughts, and I choose thoughts of strength and empowerment.

- Every decision I make is infused with power.

- I am in harmony with the universe. This harmony creates a flow of power within me that knows no bounds.

- I command my subconscious mind to manifest power in every aspect of my life. This is now my reality.

You've come now to understand your power. By activating and cultivating this power, you transform the depths remaining to be plumbed and peaks to scale. Foundations strengthened through the shared experience of rising consciousness have now been laid. Inner steadiness has nurtured and nourished each ongoing step as paths ahead now return with their many gifts. The awareness cultivated from this experience brightens all trails, and our gratitude remains that you choose to walk alongside believers in your worth and the power of your radiance. Go now in peace, assured that this infinite power is released within you.

You will notice that you're manifesting much faster as you go out into the day. Tend well the seeds sown here and spread their blossoms widely. Until our paths cross again, know that your light lights all the land it touches. The gifts freely shared shall bear fruit wherever sown in ways both seen and unseen. With rigid filters dissolved, compassions call sounds clear, and answering its summons, we attune to needs before unheard and unseen. With widened power comes the willingness to lend support wherever darkness lingers.

Who knows which tiny sparks kindle here may ignite new beacons for souls adrift, may stoke fresh courage, and those swaying on hopes precipice each radiance magnifies the hole as dropped into the ocean and in multiplying our kindled lights, how drastically futures may morph. Dark fortunes have transformed through simpler acts of shared gifts previously unseen. This work continues beyond parting, ensuring as tides rhythm may memories nurtured water, seeds of a future harvest, and hearts stay tender to life's constant changes.

Recognizing the potential in yourself and all people will guide you. Your influence expands in spirals, ever-widening, if rooted in empowering others faithfully and as you have learned to empower yourself. In this spirit, may the ripples of your power spread outward to all who need it. For with great power comes great responsibility. The ripple effect of your power will light the way for others still walking their paths. Use this power for good, and that service will be your legacy.

Your power is now activated.

YOUR POWER IS ACTIVATED

"The closer you come to knowing that you alone create the world of your experience, the more vital it becomes for you to discover just who is doing the creating."

— *Eric Micha'el Leventhal*

My intention in writing this book was to activate your power. If you have made it this far, you have unlocked this power and embraced the unique magic and magnetism you possess. Your power is officially activated. These pages were written to speak to your inner being. You may have already begun to see the effects of this in your world. Each word was crafted to awaken this inner being. Something wonderful is happening for you right now. You've been reminded of your remarkable capabilities and taught the importance of releasing what holds you back, allowing the enchantment of everyday existence to permeate your life.

It is time to let go of the past and embrace a new future with unlimited possibilities. You can do anything, experience anything, and achieve anything. Your wishes and dreams are inevitable. There is nothing stopping you. Today is your second chance, and everything is working to your advantage.

Remember, the power to create your desired reality is in your hands, and with each step, you're reshaping the world around you.

Let this serve as a reminder that the scope of your potential is boundless. I have planted seeds within your soul, destined to sprout and grow in your life. It is inevitable. Carry these teachings with you as a source of strength and inspiration, ready to face whatever comes.

Every day, I attempt to navigate the subtle whims of this power and learn and teach how to use it. So, as you move on from this book, join me on my channel, meditate with me weekly, and share your journey with me as you harness your power and craft your own story. This activation is an ongoing process, and every day, with every breath, the grandeur and magnificence of your life will expand into untold realms. There is no limit to what you can be, do, and have.

As you continue, know that the process of discovering and harnessing your power is ongoing. Your story of greatness is just beginning. Stand tall, stay empowered, and continue to shine your light on the world. The future is not just something you enter; it's something you create, and with each passing moment, you have the power to craft a reality brimming with joy, success, and fulfillment. You now have the keys to change the world. Grant yourself permission and show the world what you will do as you harness your unlimited power and discover the boundless possibilities that lie within.

Welcome to The Reality Revolution!

RECOMMENDED READING AND OTHER RESOURCES

Other Books from the Author:

In **The Reality Revolution: The Mind-Blowing Movement to Hack Your Reality**, Brian introduces you to the techniques that have helped his clients find lasting love, create wealth, and revitalize health. You'll learn how to surf through parallel realities and unlock the power of your mind through a mix of researched and science-backed techniques like qi gong, meditation, quantum jumping, energy work, and reality transurfing. If you're ready to create an incredible reality for yourself, this book shows you the way.

Websites:

https://www.therealityrevolution.com/

https://www.newearth.art/

Join the Community:

Connect with like-minded community members in the Facebook Group **Welcome to The Reality Revolution:**
https://bit.ly/TheRealityRevolutionFB

Join the email list to receive an exclusive, members-only weekly release of a new art piece or meditation.

Videos and Podcast:

Subscribe to The Reality Revolution YouTube Channel at:

https://www.youtube.com/@BrianScott1111

ABOUT THE AUTHOR

BRIAN SCOTT brings a unique blend of cutting-edge science, business savvy, and unbridled curiosity to his work. Where else can you find an NLP Master Practitioner, Certified Hypnotist, Meditation Trainer, and bookstore owner who's also a comic book fan, Pearl Jam lifer, proud father, and motivational speaker who still thinks he's an artist. Brian is the CEO of the Advanced Success Institute and host of The Reality Revolution Podcast. To learn more about Brian's work, check out TheRealityRevolution.com.

Printed in Great Britain
by Amazon